Scroll Saw

Country Patterns

Patrick Spielman &
Sherri Spielman Valitchka

Art by Dirk Boelman, The Art Factory

 Sterling Publishing Co., Inc.   New York

Copyright © 1990 by Patrick Spielman and Sherri Spielman Valitchka
Published by Sterling Publishing Co., Inc.
387 Park Avenue South, New York, N.Y. 10016
Distributed in Canada by Sterling Publishing
% Canadian Manda Group, P.O. Box 920, Station U
Toronto, Ontario, Canada M8Z 5P9
Distributed in Great Britain and Europe by Cassell PLC
Artillery House, Artillery Row, London SW1P 1RT, England
Distributed in Australia by Capricorn Ltd.
P.O. Box 665, Lane Cove, NSW 2066
Manufactured in the United States of America
All rights reserved

Spielman, Patrick B.
    Scroll saw country patterns / Patrick Spielman & Sherri Spielman
Valitchka ; final art by Dirk Boelman.
        p.   cm.
    ISBN 0-8069-7220-3
    1. Jig saws.   2. Woodwork.   I. Valitchka, Sherri Spielman.
II. Title.
TT186.S668   1990
745.51—dc20   89-78351
                                                                CIP

Table of Contents

COLOR PAGES FOLLOW PAGE 64

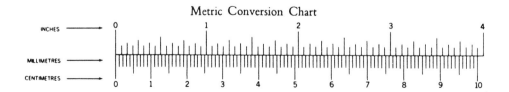

Metric Conversion Chart

Acknowledgments

We express our sincerest gratitude and appreciation to Patricia Spielman, spouse and mother, for her artistic assistance in this work. Her keen eye, sense of proportion, and exceptional design talents were called upon often to help us expedite the reality of this book.

Our very special thanks to our artist, Dirk Boelman of The Art Factory, for his design suggestions, executing quality art production, and his excellent cooperation giving us quick and vital turn around time. Thanks also goes wholeheartedly to Luke Valitchka for his support, encouragement, and his hands-on help in the workshop.

Introduction and Helpful Tips

The country look in home decorating has evolved over the last 10 to 15 years to become a standard. Country has proven to be more than a passing trend as some experts earlier predicted. Today, country designs cut out of wood are favorites among decorators, collectors, and woodworkers across North America and Europe.

Country style gives a feeling of warmth and coziness to a home. The country look contributes to the homeowner's sense of peace and serenity away from his daily struggles with the masses, the cold plastics, and high tech environments of the work place. People want to see and touch real wood. They like one-of-a-kind objects, hand-made works that are special and uniquely different from mass produced products.

All this is good news for the scroll saw woodworker. Country cut-outs are fun, fast and easy to do. Making these objects requires no great artistic or special mechanical aptitudes. The necessary sawing skills are learned quickly. (See Illus. 1.) Anyone above the age of nine can soon learn to make objects for their own use and pleasure, or for giving and/or to sell for fair profits.

Also on the list of good news for the scroll saw owner are some new machine developments and a number of tips and shortcuts that greatly simplify the work. The new "constant tension" scroll saws manufactured in the last dozen or so years make accurate, detailed cutting of thicker materials faster and easier than ever before possible. (See Illus. 1.)

All of the patterns in this book can be cut with any scroll or jig saw. Many patterns can also be cut with a band saw. However, generally speaking, scroll saws cut almost as fast as band saws and they are much safer. They can also cut sharper turns and saw out inside openings, making them well-suited for smaller work such as these patterns. To use these patterns, you'll need to transfer them from the page to your work, and for this you first need a copy of the pattern. It's easy to find a paper that is sufficiently transparent so you can trace over the dark black outlines of the patterns. An office copy machine, however, makes quick work of this step. Pattern copies can also be enlarged or reduced to practically any predetermined size on many machines. Copiers are becoming more and more sophisticated and also accessible to almost everyone. Most public libraries have them as do most quick printing establishments for individuals to use. Many businesses and schools, even in remote, rural towns and villages, often make them available for public use on a cost per copy basis. Pattern copies of any size can now be made in just seconds for pennies a copy. Gone are those labor intensive and crude copying and enlarging techniques using graph grids, difficult to adjust pantographs, or methods of tracing off of various illuminated projection devices.

Now all that is needed is an easy, speedy, and accurate method of transferring the copied pattern to the work piece. To satisfy this important requirement, we highly recommend a spray adhesive to bond the pattern directly onto the wood, such as 3-M's Scotch Brand Spray Mount Artist's Adhesive (catalog #6065.) Most photography stores and studios carry this as do art,

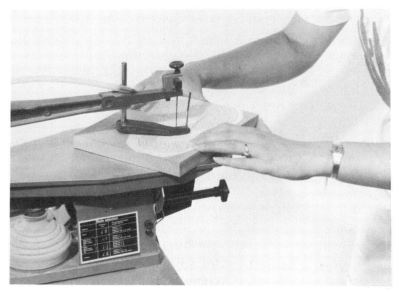

Illus. 1

Any small scroll saw can be used to make most of the projects in this book. Here 1" thick wood is cut with a narrow blade.

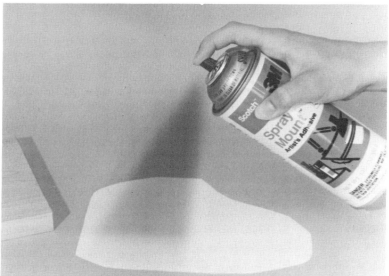

Illus. 2

Apply a very light coating of spray mount adhesive to the back of the pattern.

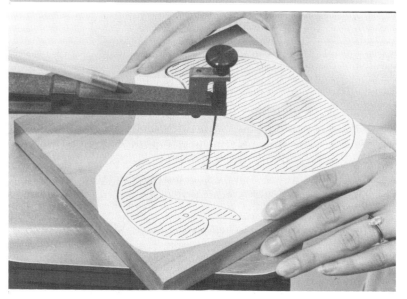

Illus. 3

The copied pattern hand-pressed onto the wood eliminates the need for tracing with messy carbons.

graphics, and craft supply stores. One can, costing under $10.00, will last the average scroll sawyer about 1 year, and is a superb material.

To use the adhesive, simply apply a very light mist to the back of the pattern copy. (See Illus. 2.) Wait 15 to 30 seconds and press the pattern copy onto your wood with hand pressure and, presto!—you're ready to begin sawing. (See Illus. 3.) Gone are the frustrations of doing tracings, working with carbon papers and similar techniques that never really produced clear, crisp, or accurate layout lines which are obviously so essential to good sawing. When sawing is completed, the pattern is easily peeled off. (See Illus. 4.) The adhesive leaves virtually no residue on the wood that might inhibit subsequent finishing. We feel obligated, by tradition I suppose, to sand the wood surface with just a few strokes of 220 abrasive before finishing, but it's really doubtful if this is even necessary.

We have made a serious effort to provide a fresh, new selection of scroll saw patterns in this book to complement those of our other pattern books, including the new *Spielman's Original Scroll Saw Patterns*. The fine, crisp lines with extra shading should help let you know where and where not to drill or saw. This we feel also helps to relieve eye strain and contributes to easier and more accurate cutting. We have included almost 400 patterns in 28 different categories. Our intent is to provide a wide range of new projects, from fairly simple ones to those of intermediate challenge level. Overall, in terms of difficulty the patterns in this book fall somewhere in between those in our *Scroll Saw Pattern Book* and *Scroll Saw Fretwork Techniques And Patterns*, prepared with professional scroll sawyer, James Reidle.

Try to visualize the many ways a single pattern, of your liking, can be used. This will multiply the value of this book and the number of projects you can make with one pattern. Although not fully illustrated here, think about using various pattern designs

as wall hangings, shelf or mantle decorations, as door stops, tree or window ornaments, paper weights, key chains, miniatures and jewelry, refrigerator magnets, or just add pegs (Illus. 5) or hooks to hang things on. Think of the designs used as overlay or pierced decorations glued on to plaques, cabinet doors and panels, on jewelry boxes and ornamentation on wood signs to name just a few more application possibilities. Flip-flop the design or cut them in pairs and make a row of the same pattern. Or, for even more variety, cut the same pattern from different materials.

Most of the patterns can be sawn from materials of your choice of species, type, and thickness. For your information, we have indicated the materials we used to make the projects illustrated in the color section. These are only suggestions. Where specific dimensions or finishes are important to a project pattern, they are included. Many of the projects can be sawn either from any solid wood or from a plywood you might choose in any thickness from 1/32 inch to 2¾ inch or more—whatever is your preference or is dictated by the capacity of your scroll saw.

Piercing and *inside cutting* is a necessary technique for cutting out openings and to do line work detailing. Piercing requires drilling a very small hole(s) to permit the blade (No. 4 or 5) to be threaded through the work. (See Illus. 6 and 7.) Once the blade is again clamped on each end in the machine and tensioned, sawing can proceed as usual until the inside opening work is completed. The piercing technique is also an effective way of using the scroll saw to cut away a single inside line. Sawing a line through the thickness of the work will dramatically accentuate the design detail intended on many patterns.

Stack cutting or *plural sawing* involves layering two or more pieces on top of each other and sawing them simultaneously. This results in perfectly identical sawn parts. (See Illus. 8.) Stack cutting is a good technique to employ to increase produc-

Illus. 4

After sawing is completed, the pattern lifts off the wood easily, leaving no residue to interfere with finishing.

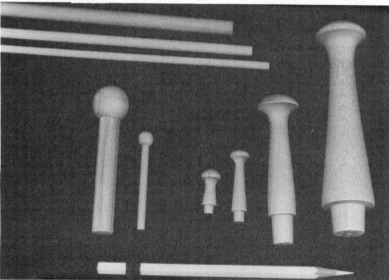

Illus. 5

Dowels and pegs are available in a variety of sizes.

Illus. 6

A combination pierce cutting and stack cutting operation in progress. Holes are drilled to permit the blade to be threaded through the wood to saw out the openings. Two layers are stacked and nailed together in the waste area to produce identically sawn designs.

Illus. 7

The inside piercing cuts are made before sawing the outside profile cut, which when completed frees both pieces from each other.

Illus. 8

The result is one pattern used to cut two identical designs for the same project.

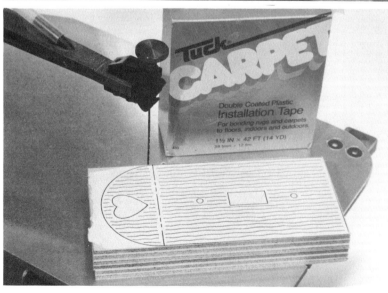

Illus. 9

Stack sawing six layers of plywood at once speeds production. The layers are held together with small pieces of double-faced tape.

Illus. 10

Penetrating danish oil is easy to use for natural or stained finishes.

Illus. 11

Some basic finishes for country projects. Some are easier to use than others. Sealers are used to minimize colored top coat penetration. Acrylic colors can be partially wiped off to effect an old, worn or antique look.

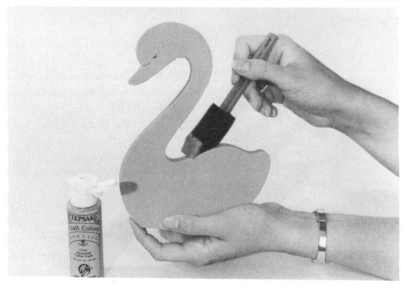

Illus. 12

Applying acrylic country colors is easy with foam brushes, and they clean-up with water.

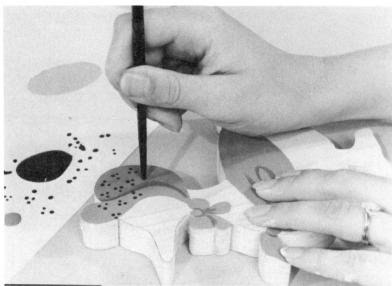

Illus. 13

Single dots in a row or a series of dots in a group can add a decorative pattern or border. Use the pointed handle end of an artists brush dipped in paint to dab uniform dots.

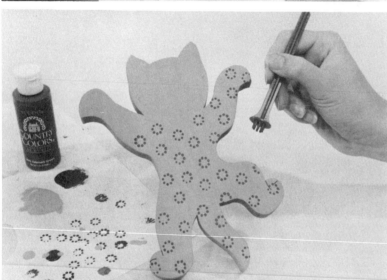

Illus. 14

This dotting tool is one of many different tools available to make decorating quick and easy. Inexpensive tools of this type are available from Meisel Hardware Specialties, Box 70, Mound, MN 55364.

Illus. 15

A couple of easy decorating techniques. Speckle finish at right is achieved by spattering on a contrasting color with the aid of a stiff bristle tooth brush. Bows, yarn, ribbon, and strings glued or hung on country animals give the object a personality of its own.

tion. The essential requirement is that the work pieces be temporarily secured to each other so they don't slip around during sawing. Various methods are used. Nailing or spot gluing in the waste area (if you have a waste area) works well when sawing thicker size stock. (See Illus. 8.) Spot gluing with just a little hot melt permits later separation.

Double-faced tape (Illus. 9) is also handy for stack cutting. You can make your own double-faced tape by using scraps of paper coated on both sides with the spray adhesive (Illus. 2) that you use to apply patterns to your work piece. This technique works great for holding layers together of all materials including those too thin to nail effectively. Spray-coated paper has more than sufficient sheer strength so the layers won't slip. On the other hand, it has a very low peel resistance which allows the layers to be separated very easily when sawing is finished. Commercially produced double-faced tape has a very aggressive tack and occasionally leaves some sticky stuff on the surface and sometimes it will pull fibers and splinters up with it. In some situations masking tape, filament tape or other types can be wrapped around stacked pieces.

Finishing. The country look often combines natural light colored or bleached woods with blue, white, and yellow painted accents. Light reddish pastels and even pinks along with natural woods are now popular. Natural woods combined with patterned papers or fabrics are also popular. Small floral prints or thin stripes of sharply contrasting colors make good accents when glued onto or displayed with wood.

Penetrating natural oil finishes such as the popular Deft and Watco brands (Illus. 10) are ideal for natural woods. If you've never used this type of finish, give it a try. Pigmented acrylic finishes are great for coloring and adding details. (See Illus. 11, 12, and 13.) Imaginative ideas can be worked up to make fairly uninteresting cut outs come alive with attractive personalities. Repetitive, contrasting dot patterns painted over a solid colored surface is one useful technique. (See Illus. 13, 14, and 15.)

Segmentation is simply sawing the pattern into various parts and then gluing them all back together. (See Illus. 16.) This is an especially useful technique that can be employed to simplify finishing while creating an unusually attractive effect. To create segmented projects the design is sawn into individual parts or pieces. (See Illus. 17.) The edges of each part should be softened or rounded over to accent the joint when the parts are reassembled. This can be accomplished by using sandpaper on small projects, (Illus. 18) or a carving knife and sandpaper and/or a router on projects having much larger pieces. The individual parts are best colored different shades before they are reassembled. Coloring can be accomplished by using pigmented oil finishes, oil stains, dyes or pigmented finishes.

Illus. 16

Examples of segmentation. The whole is sawn into individual parts (which can be shaped by sanding or rounding over). Each piece is stained or painted individually and then all parts are glued back together.

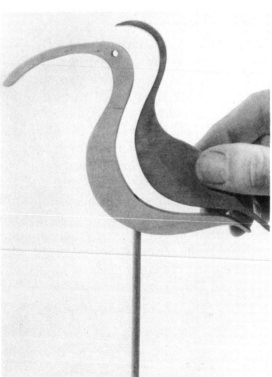

Illus. 17

A simple two-piece segmentation project. The upper part is stained and then glued back to the other unstained piece to create an attractive two-tone effect.

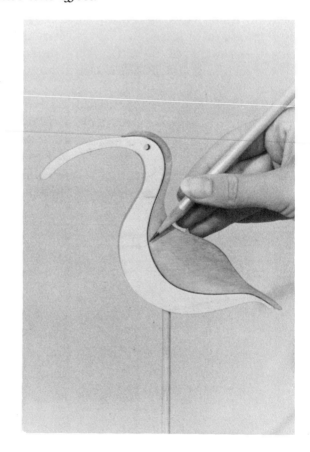

Illus. 18

Slightly rounding the sawn edges at the joint with sandpaper before staining makes for a better looking finished product.

Country Miniatures

MILK

Sheep, Lambs, and Goats

Cows

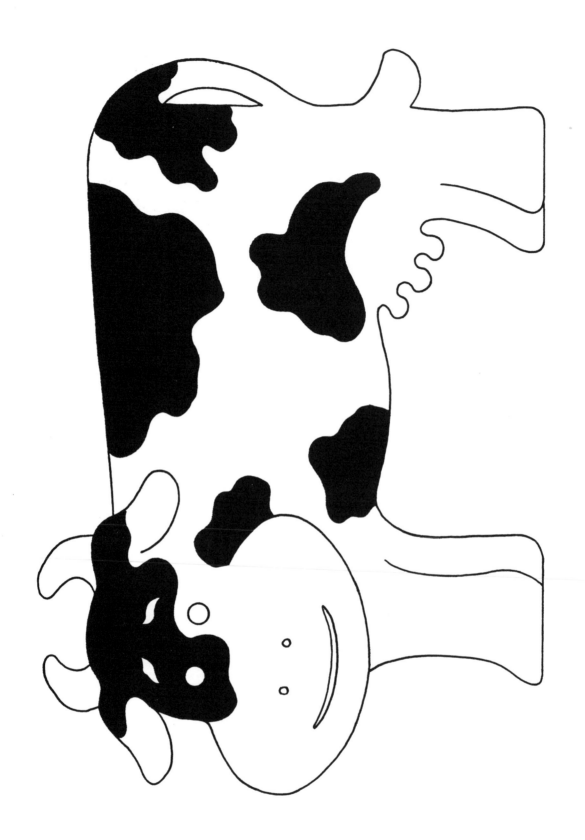

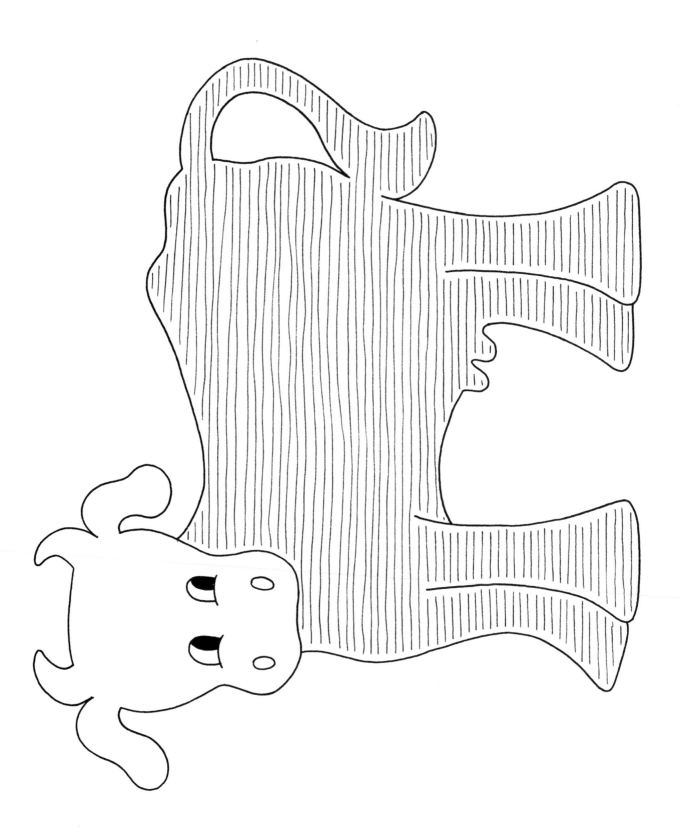

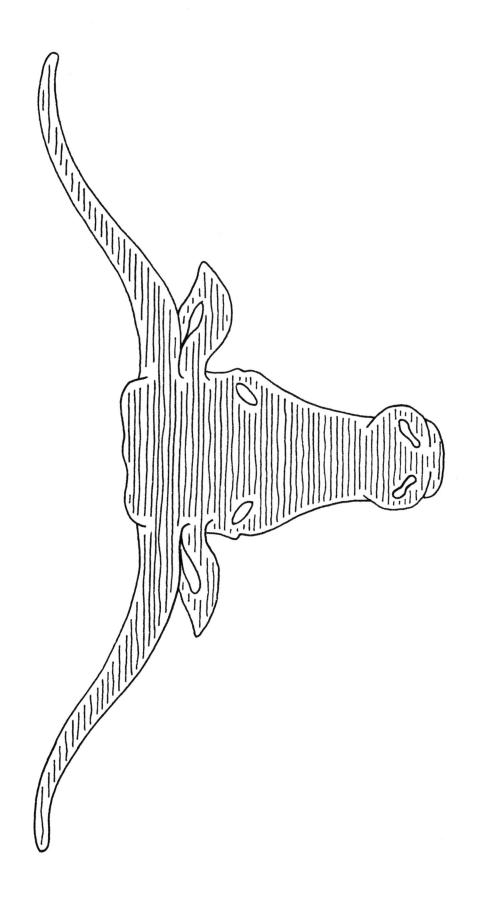

People

Boy & girl sawn from ¾" thick wood.

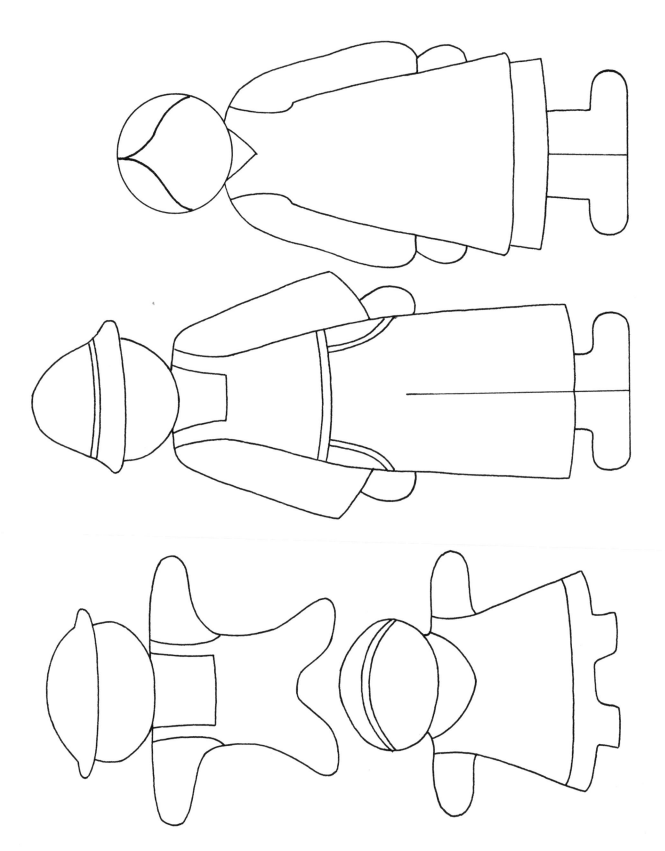

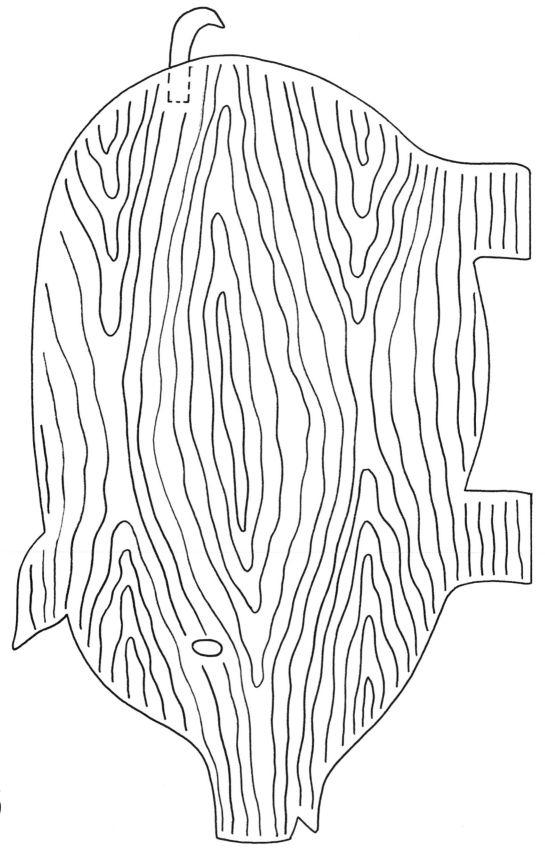

Pigs

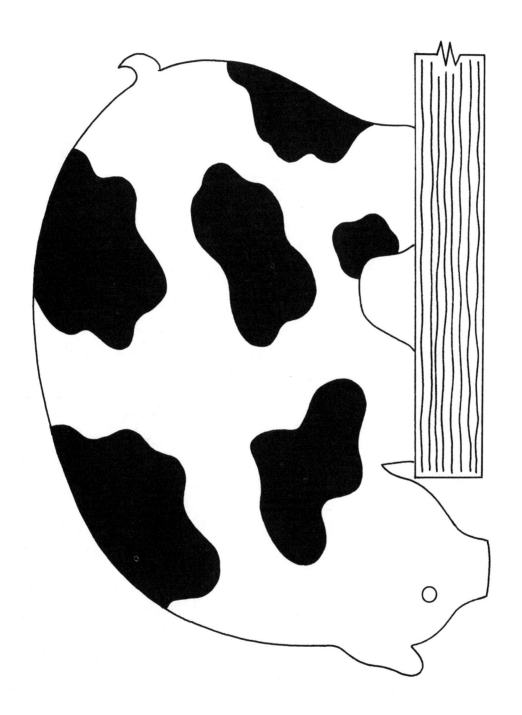

Horses

Cats

Cat and mouse are cut from ¾" thick stock. The mouse has a leather tail.

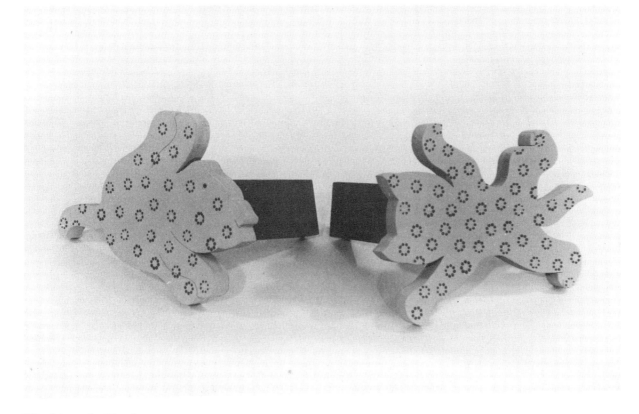

Climbing shelf cats.

OVERLAY

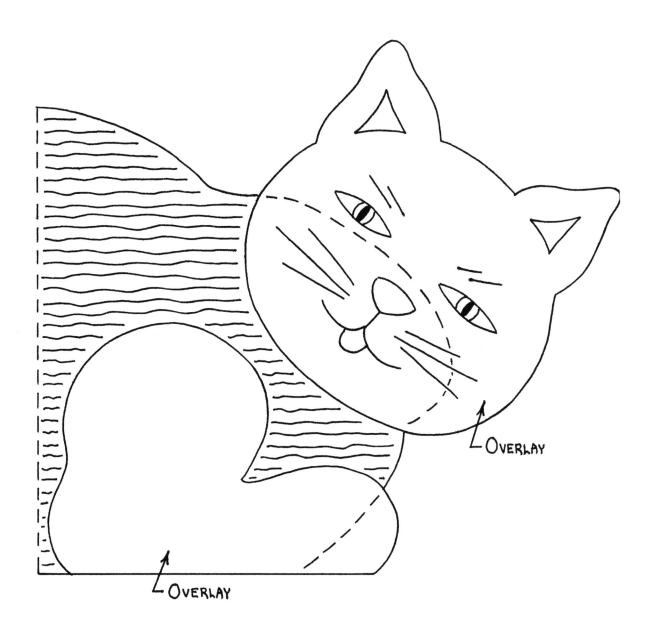

Overlay

Overlay

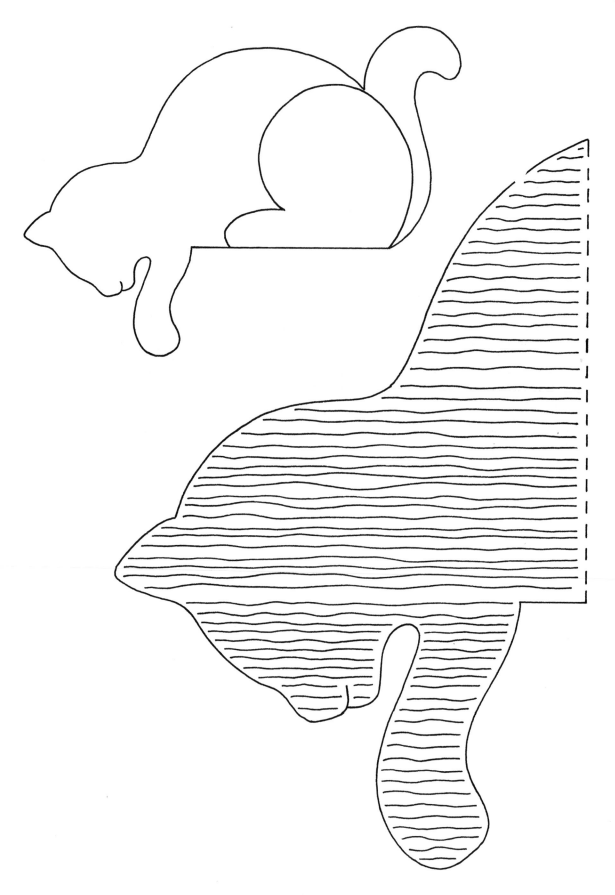

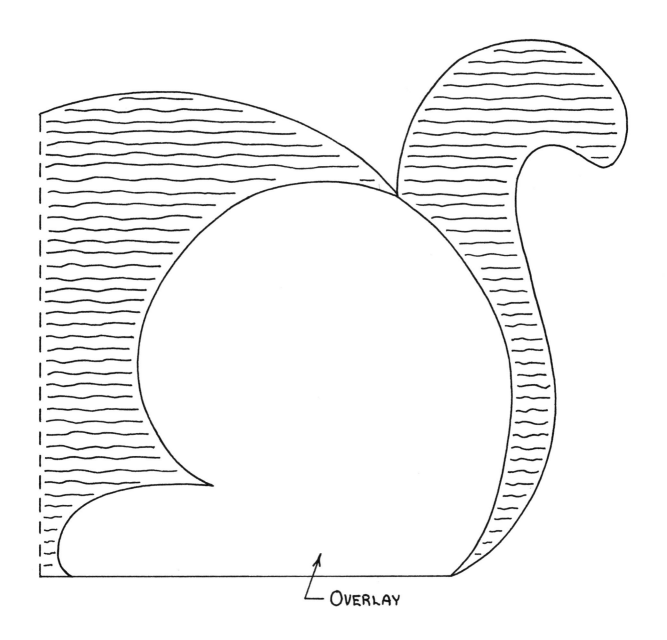

Overlay

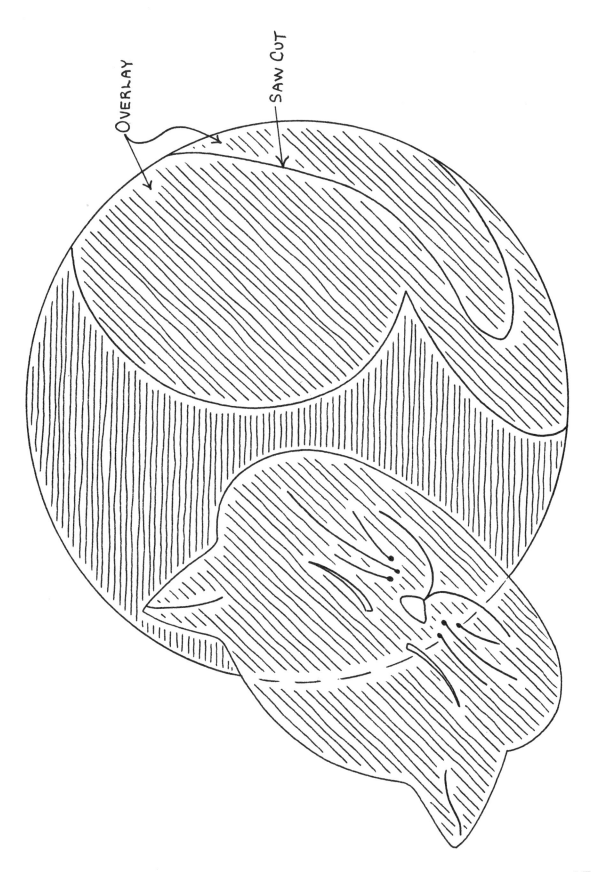

OVERLAY

SAW CUT

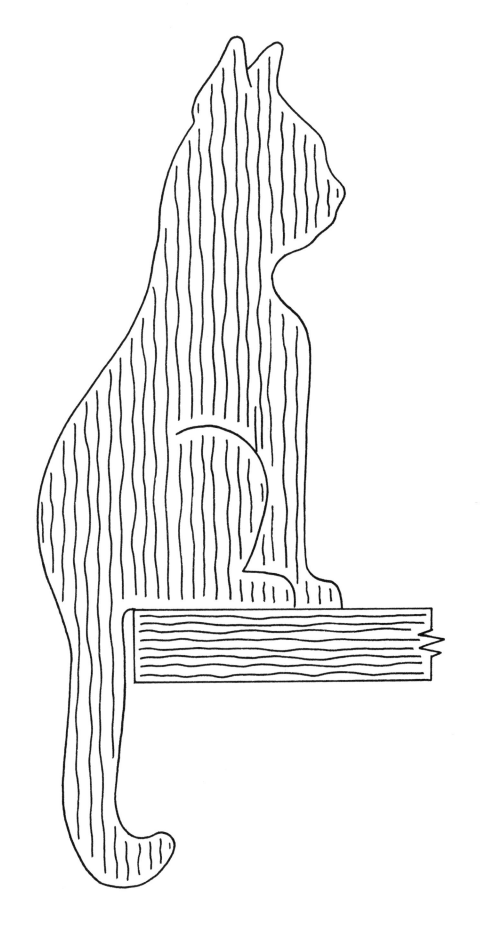

Block,
$\frac{3}{4}" \times 1\frac{3}{4}" \times 5"$

Block,
$\frac{3''}{4}$ x $1\frac{3''}{4}$ x 5"

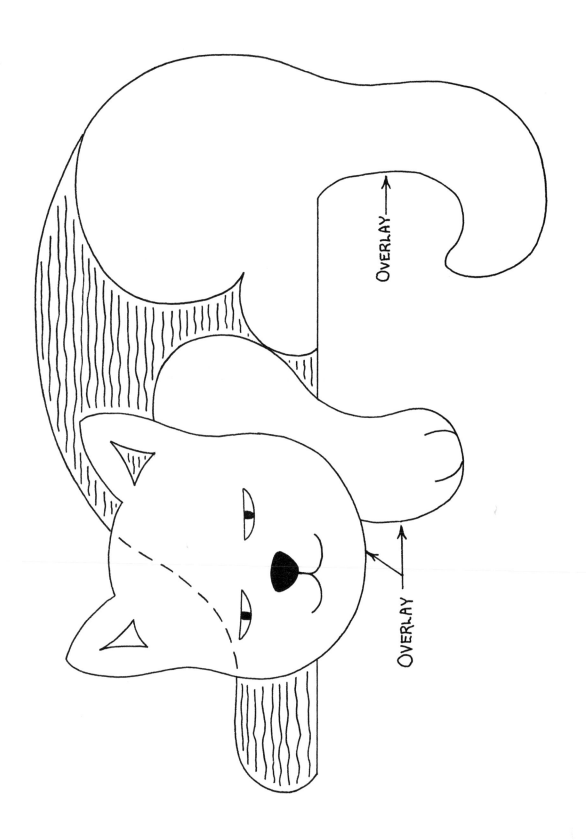

OVERLAY →

OVERLAY →

Mice

Bears

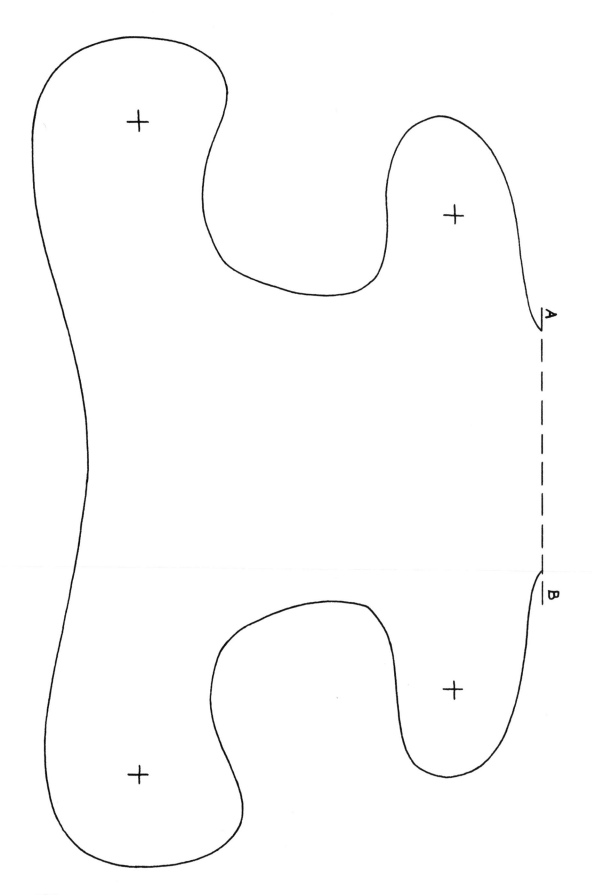

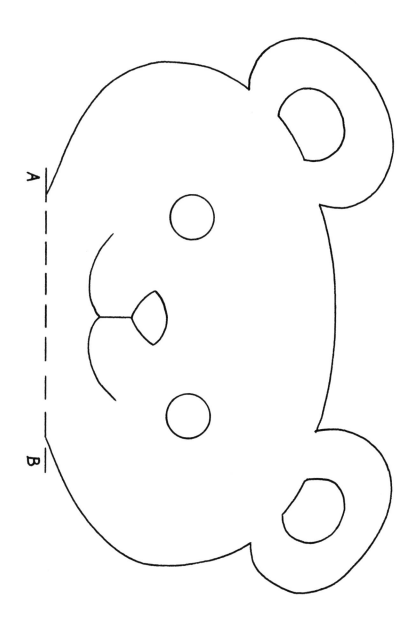

A

B

57

Welcome

A - - - - B

A - - - - B

A -------- B

Bunnies

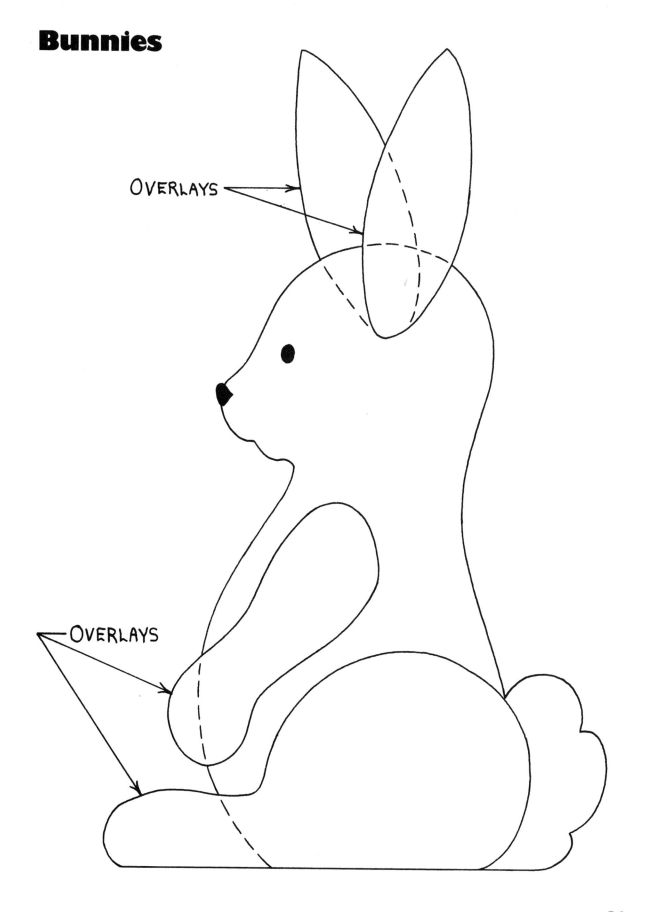

OVERLAYS

OVERLAYS

A simple cutout of pine, 1⅛" thick.

A special shelf for miniatures and small collectibles.

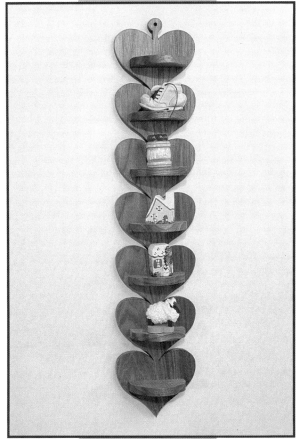

This holder for long wooden matches is a practical and decorative project.

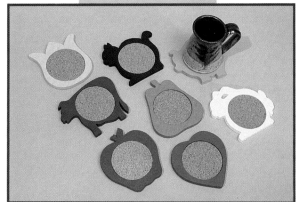

Each of these coasters is made from two layers of ¼" plywood with a ⅛" thick cork inlay.

These easy-to-make projects are finished with popular country colors and decorated with ribbons and bows.

Examples of basic scroll saw segmentation projects. The individual parts are cut free, the edges rounded, and the parts stained various colors. The pieces are then glued back together to form the original profile.

Sheep and cow sawn from ¾" wood.

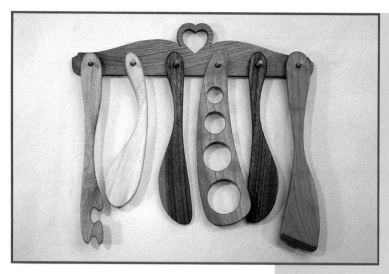

Make these wooden kitchen utensils and the special rack from thin hardwoods.

A fretted box to hold flowers, cards, and other practical or decorative items.

"Shelf Cats" and other easy and fun-to-make-and-finish cutouts.

c

Paper towel dispenser designed and made by Sally and Charles Clements.

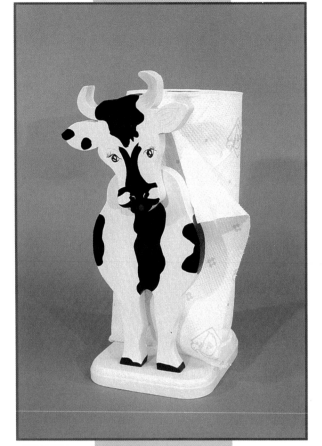

Little people cutouts made from ¾" wood and details painted with country acrylics.

Cat and mouse cut from ¾" thick material.

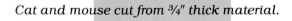

This project has an antique-looking finish that is easy to achieve.

D

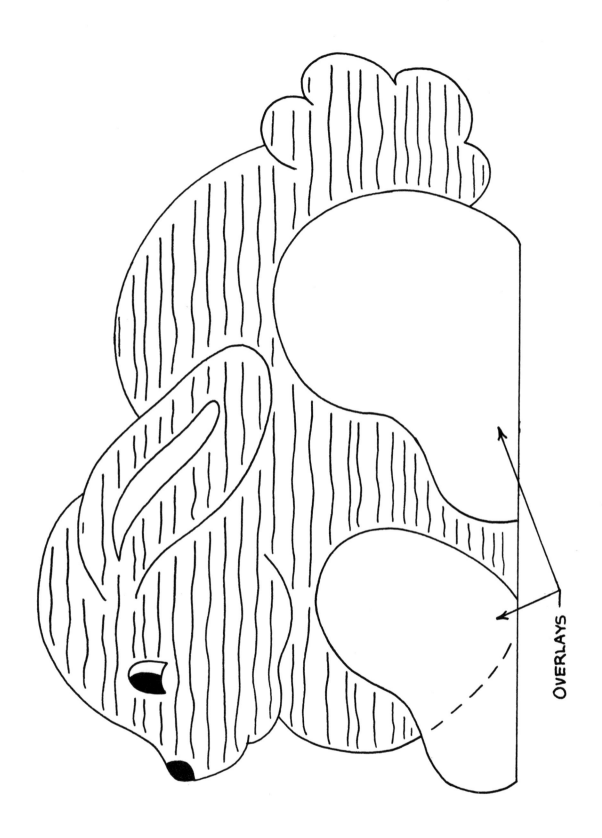

OVERLAYS

65

Birds, Butterflies, and Chickens

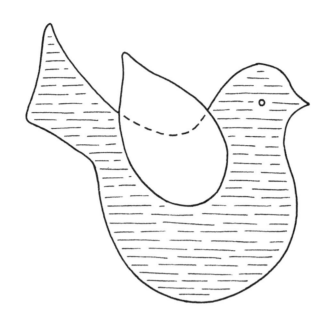

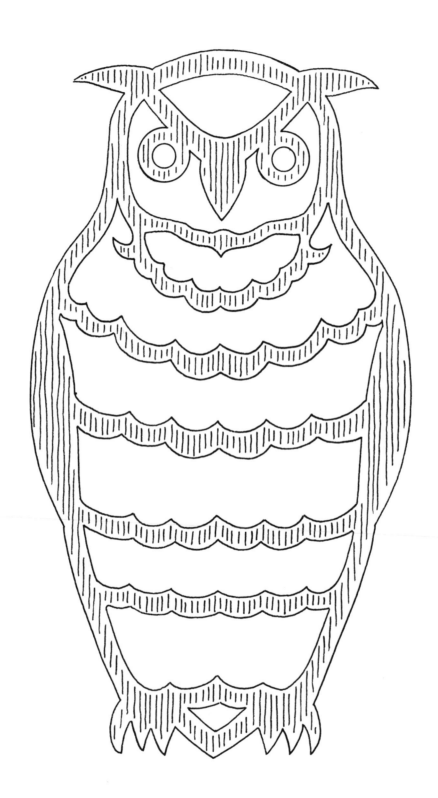

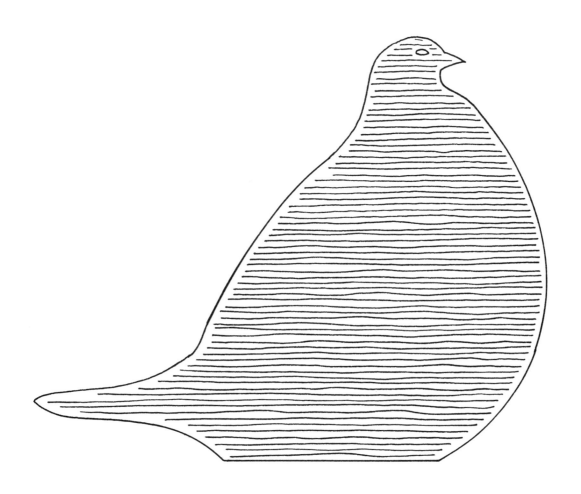

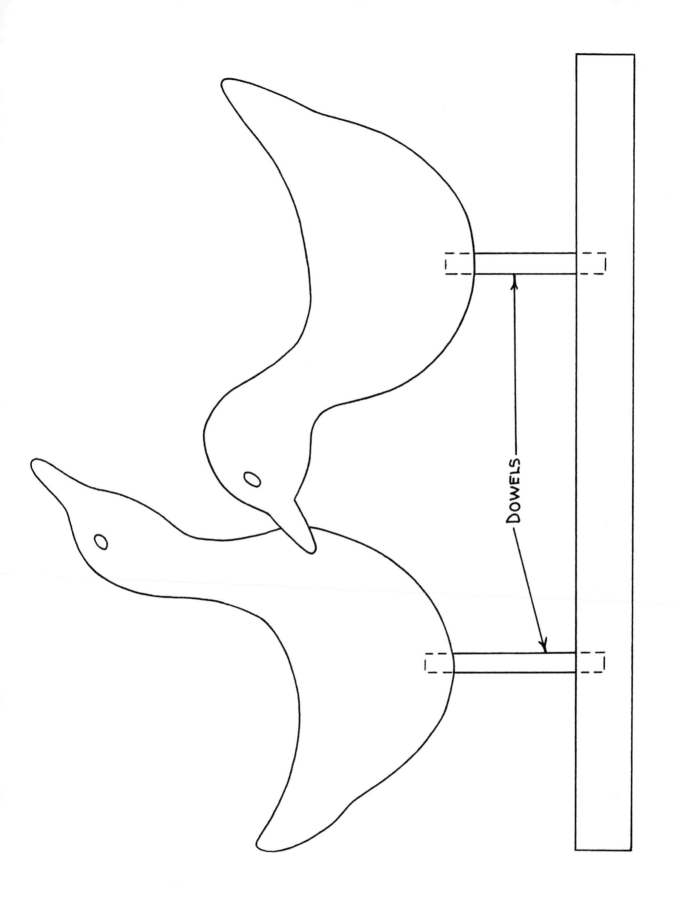

DOWELS

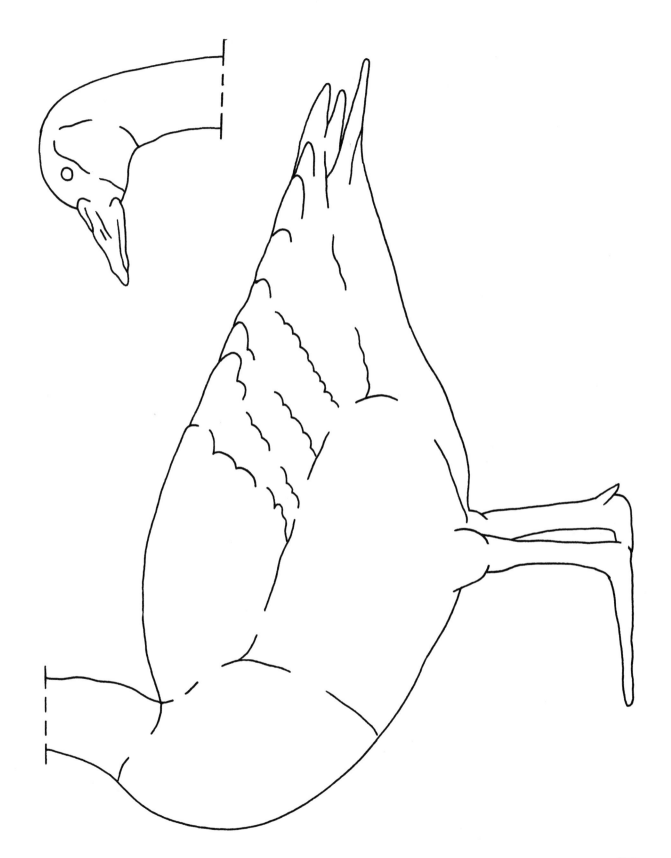

76

OVERLAY

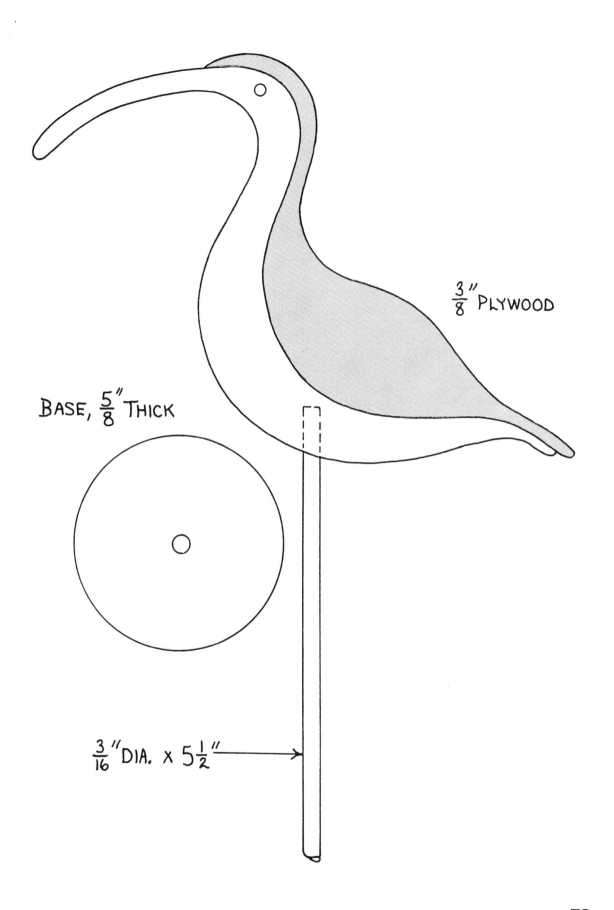

$\frac{3}{8}''$ PLYWOOD

BASE, $\frac{5}{8}''$ THICK

$\frac{3}{16}''$ DIA. x $5\frac{1}{2}''$

Geese, Swans, and Ducks

Bows or ribbons enhance otherwise plain figures.

Shore bird sawn from ½" thick Baltic birch plywood. Duck is from 1½" thick solid pine. After segmenting, the pieces were rounded over, stained, and glued back together.

The same inlay design covered with fabric.

Pierce-cut design in ³/₄″ thick butternut is rounded over and replaced so that it stands out ¼″ in relief.

Nail a wedge to the back and you've got a door stop. (See pages 100–101.)

Rear view, showing the bead of hot glue applied around the relief inlay.

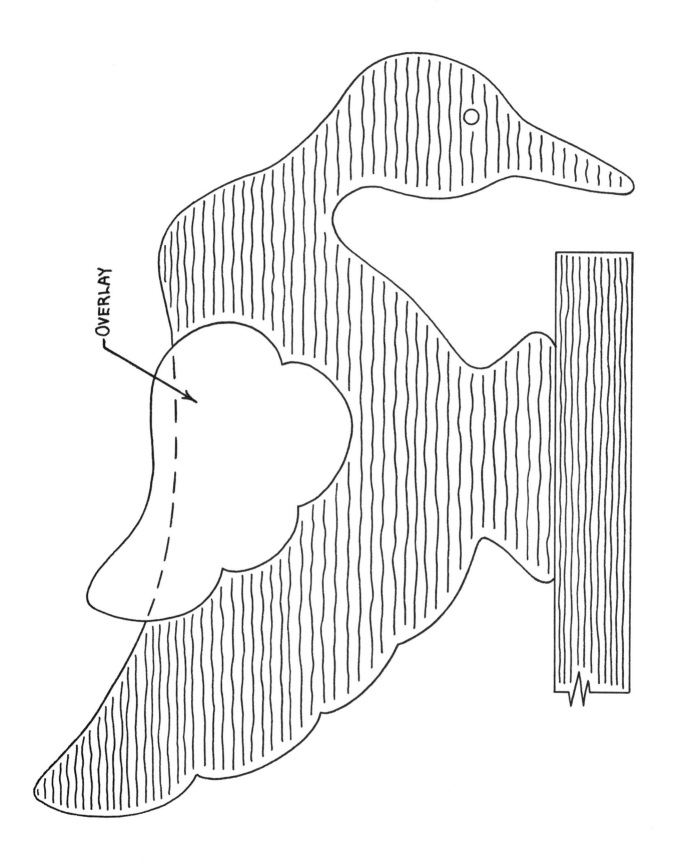

OVERLAY

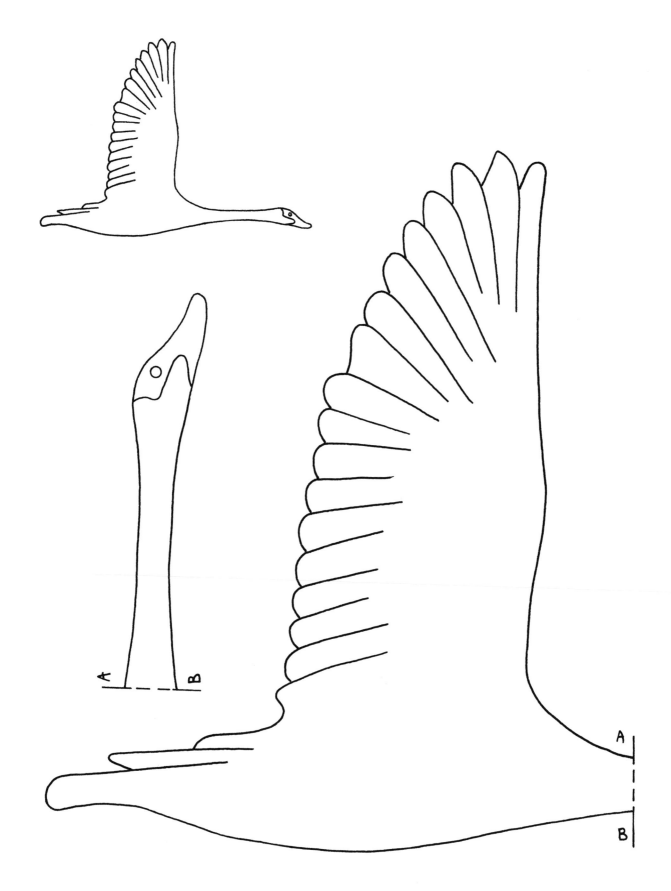

A

B

A

B

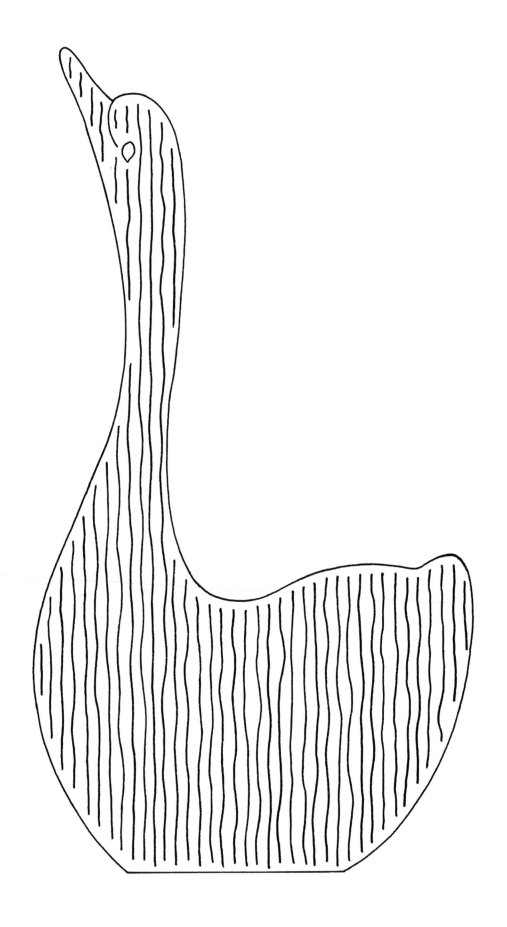

88

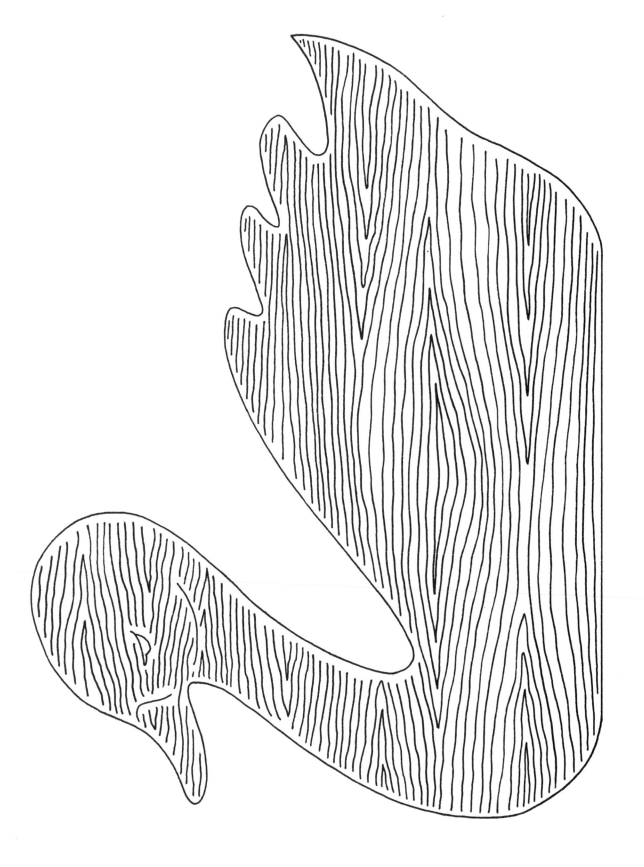

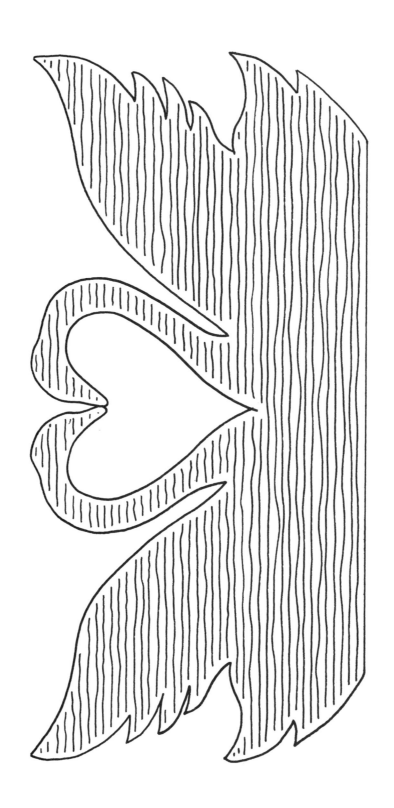

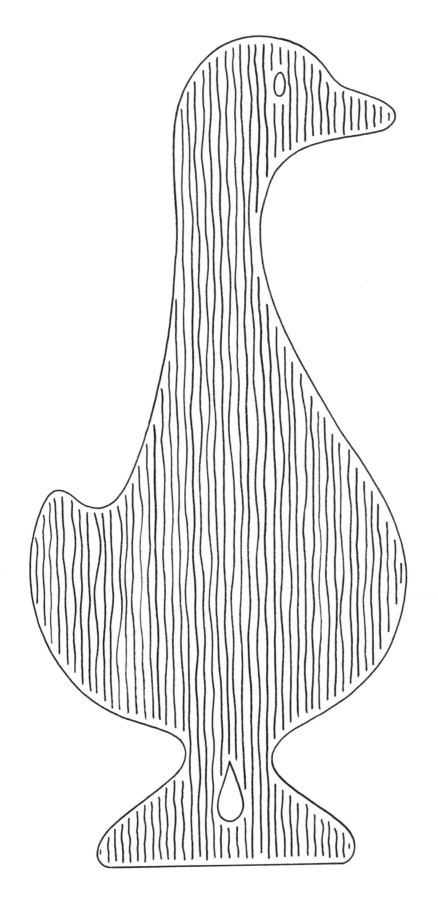

95

OVERLAY

96

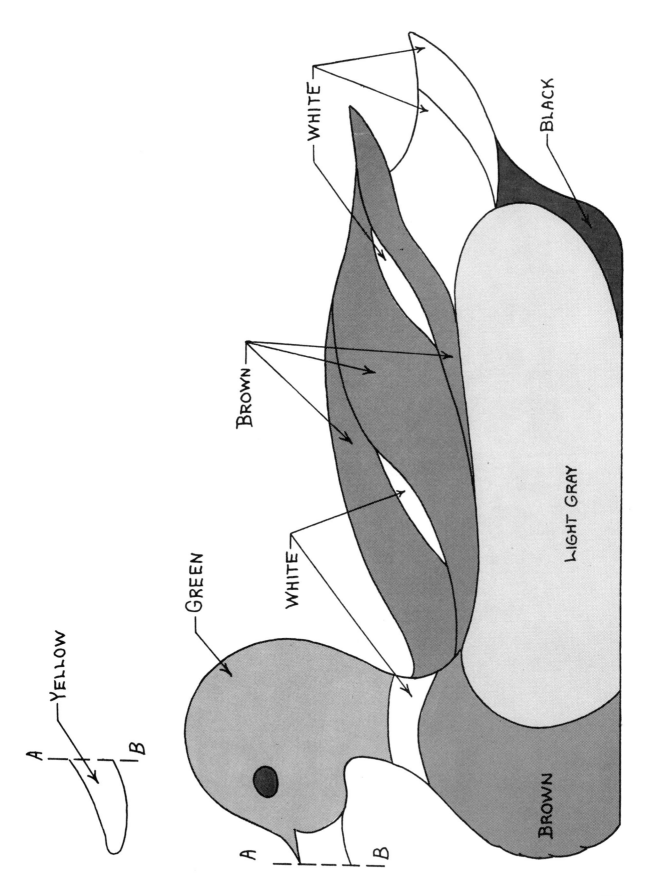

YELLOW

A

B

GREEN

WHITE

A

B

WHITE

BROWN

WHITE

BLACK

LIGHT GRAY

BROWN

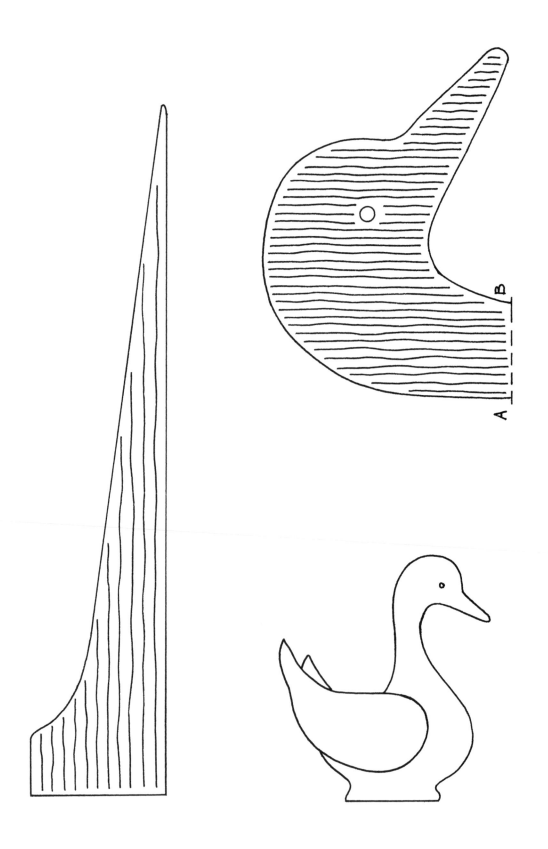

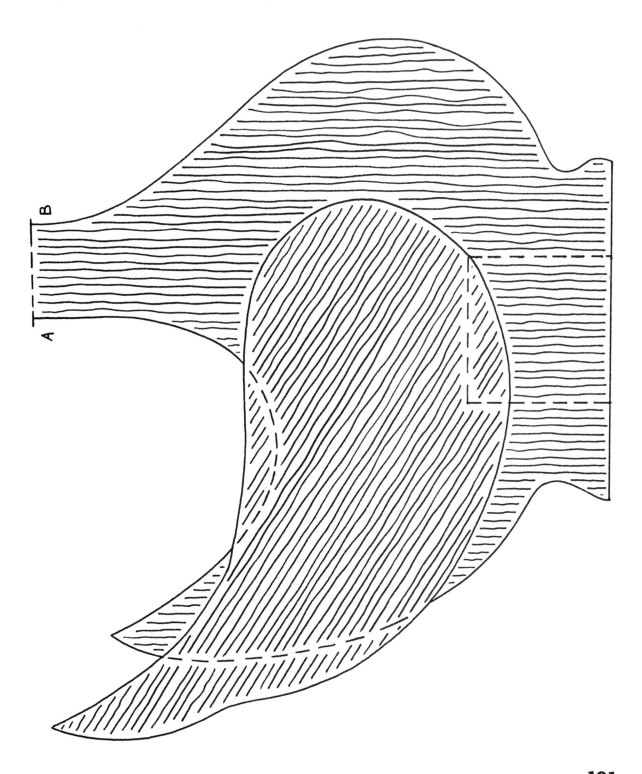

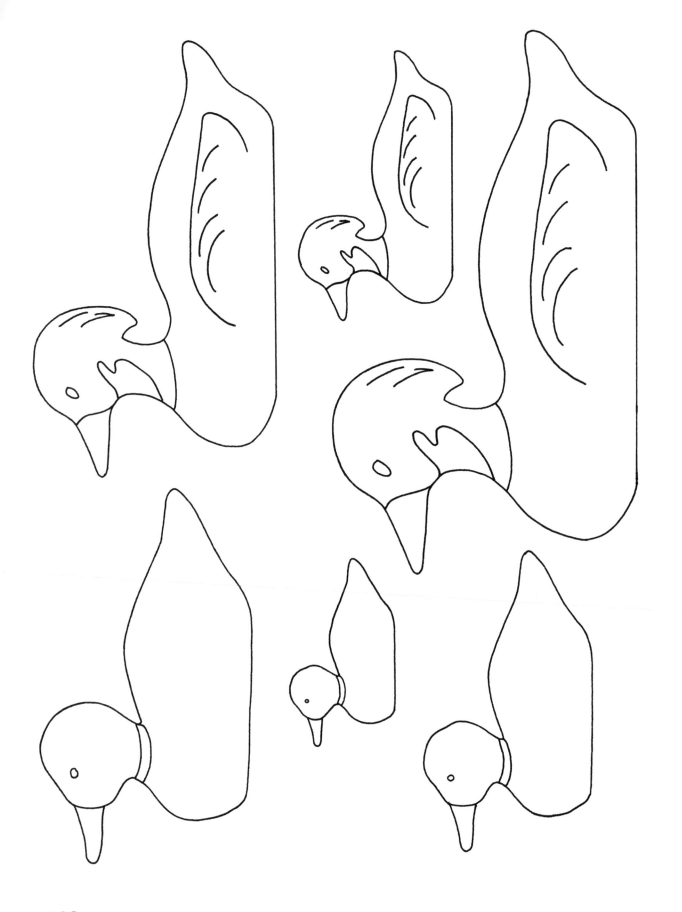

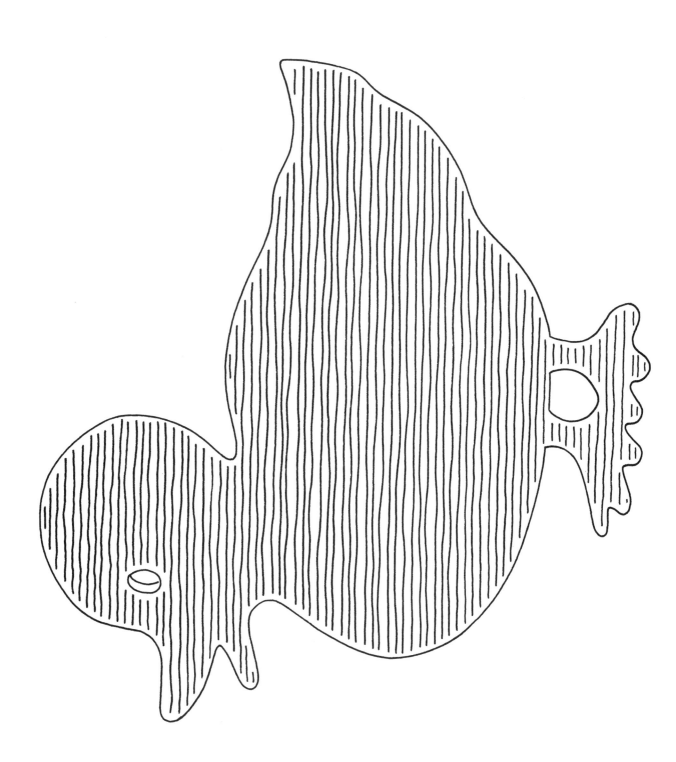

Country Hearts

A — — — — — — — — — — — B

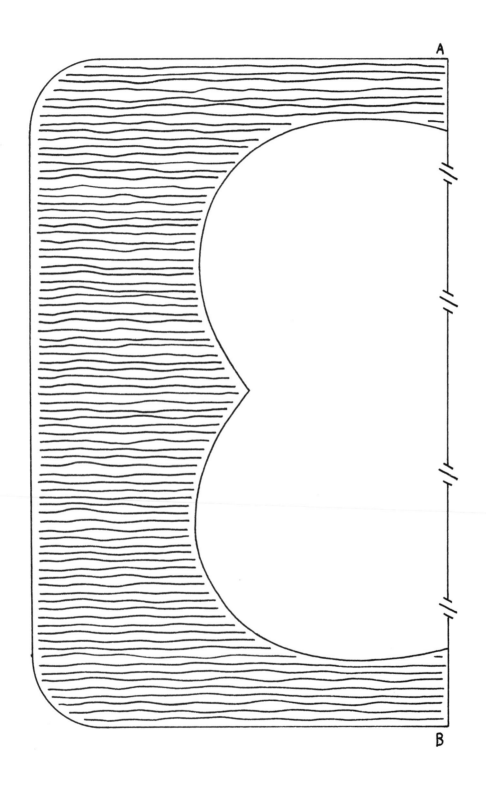

A

B

109

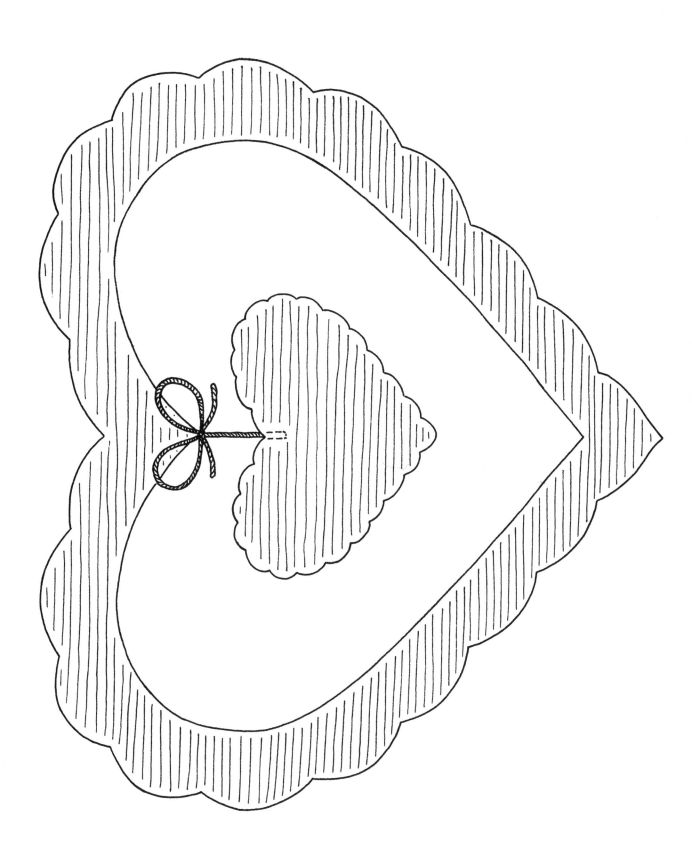

Miscellaneous Cut Outs

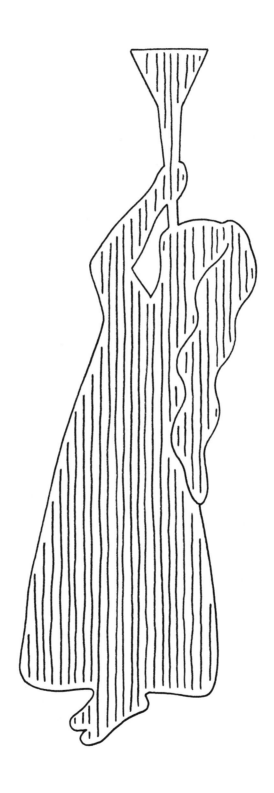

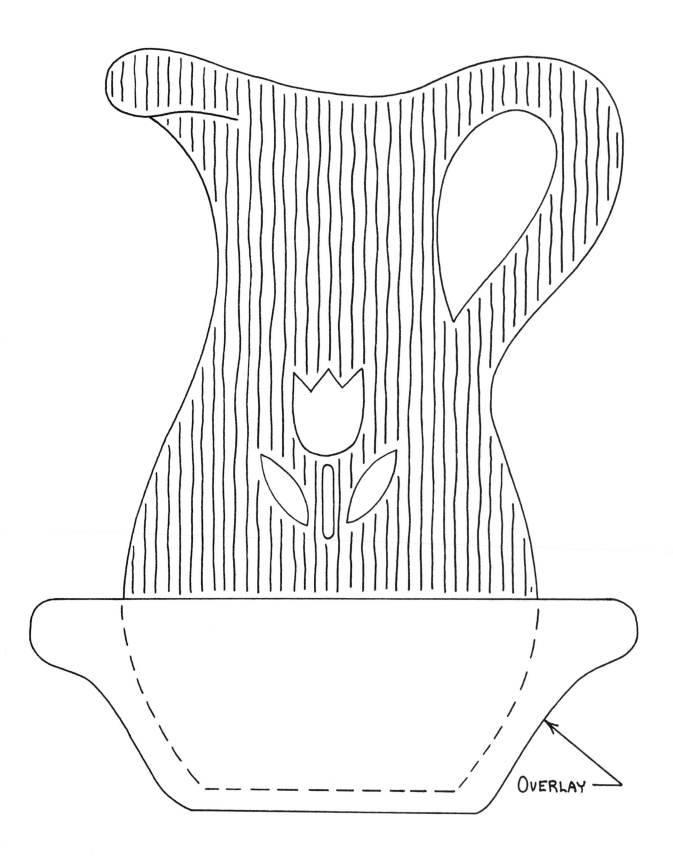

OVERLAY

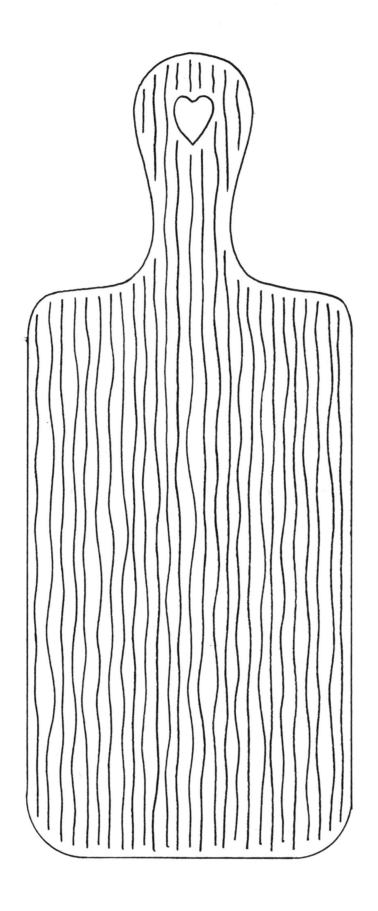

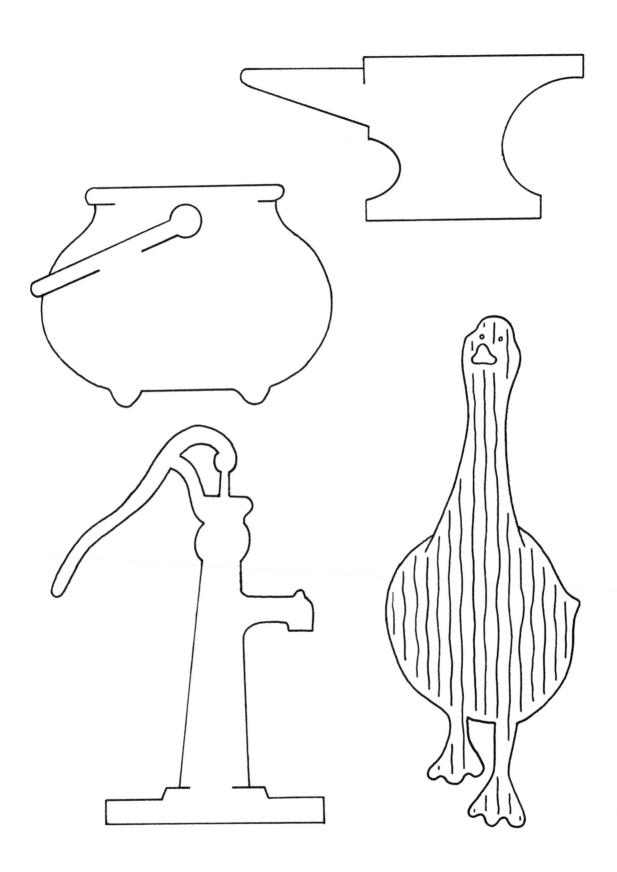

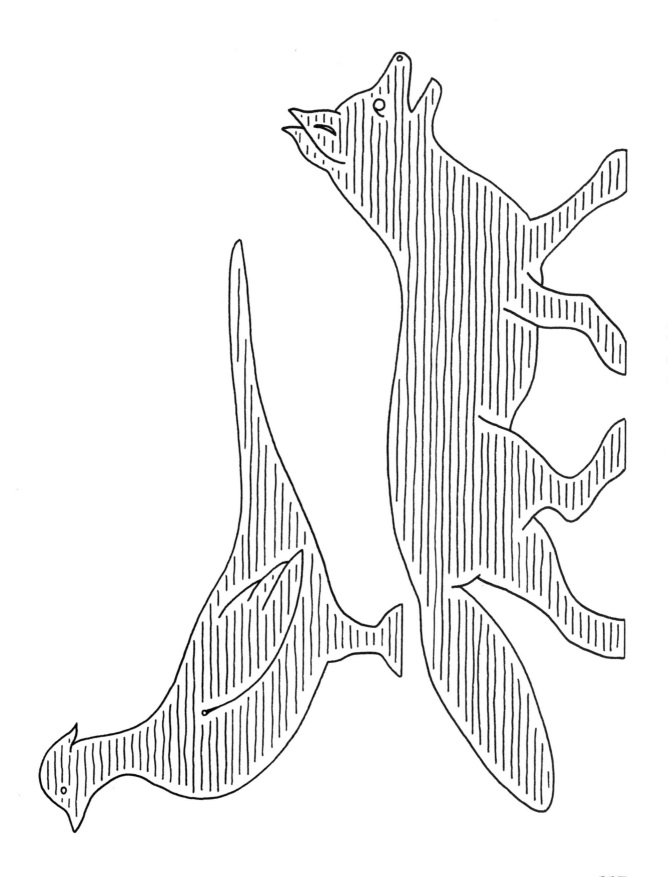

Stacked Animals

A — — B

Candle Holders

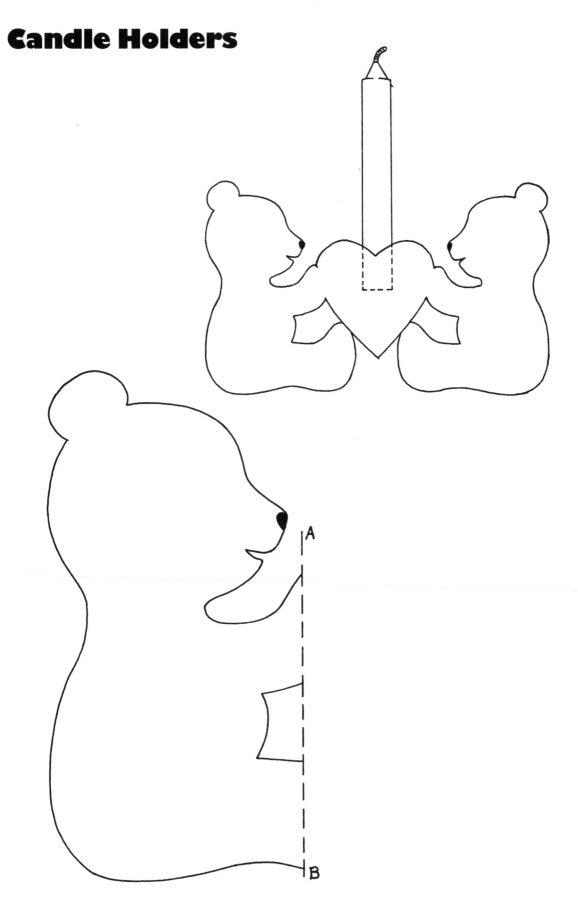

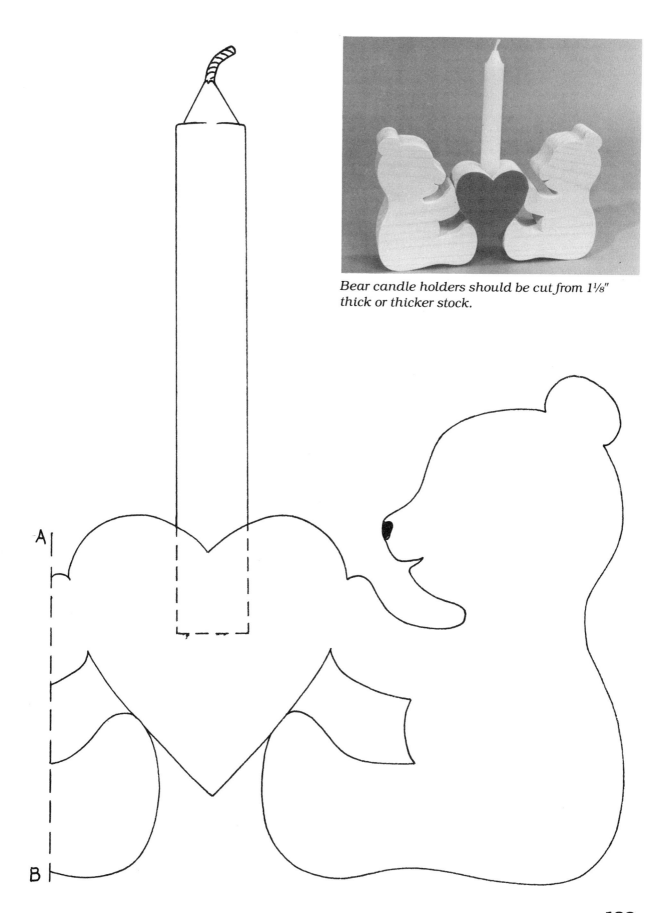

*Bear candle holders should be cut from 1⅛"
thick or thicker stock.*

A

B

123

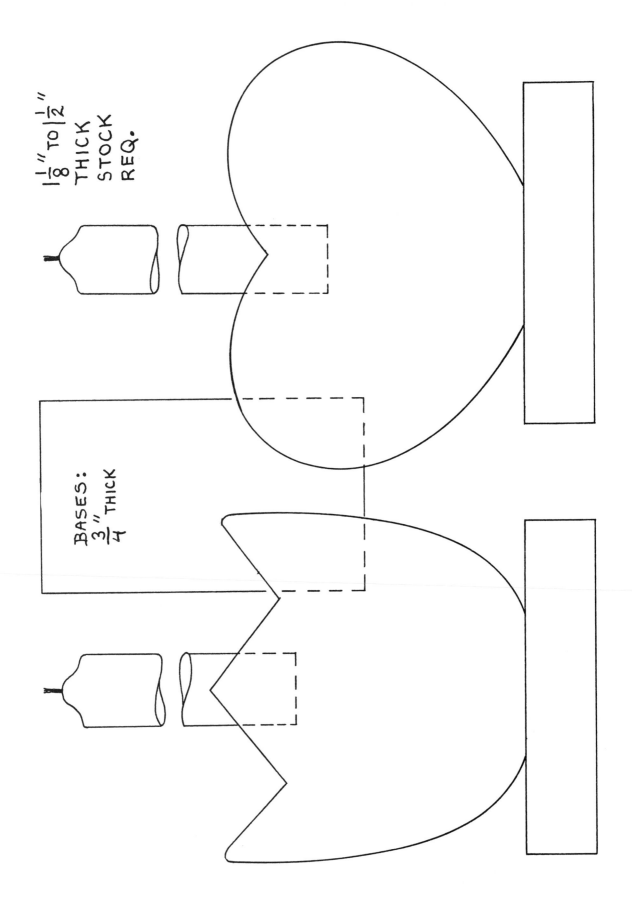

$1\frac{1}{8}''$ TO $1\frac{1}{2}''$ THICK STOCK REQ.

BASES: $\frac{3}{4}''$ THICK

Towel Holder

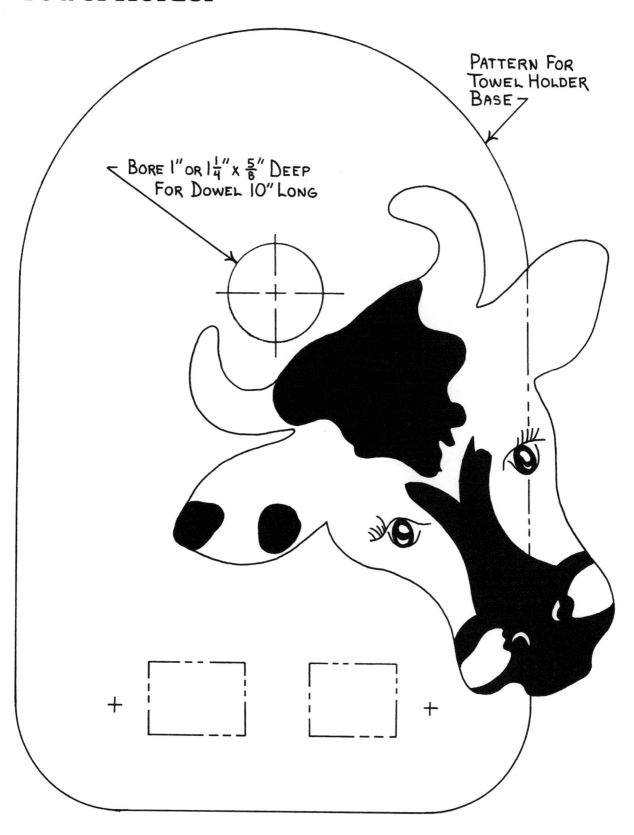

PATTERN FOR TOWEL HOLDER BASE

← BORE 1" OR 1¼" x ⅝" DEEP FOR DOWEL 10" LONG

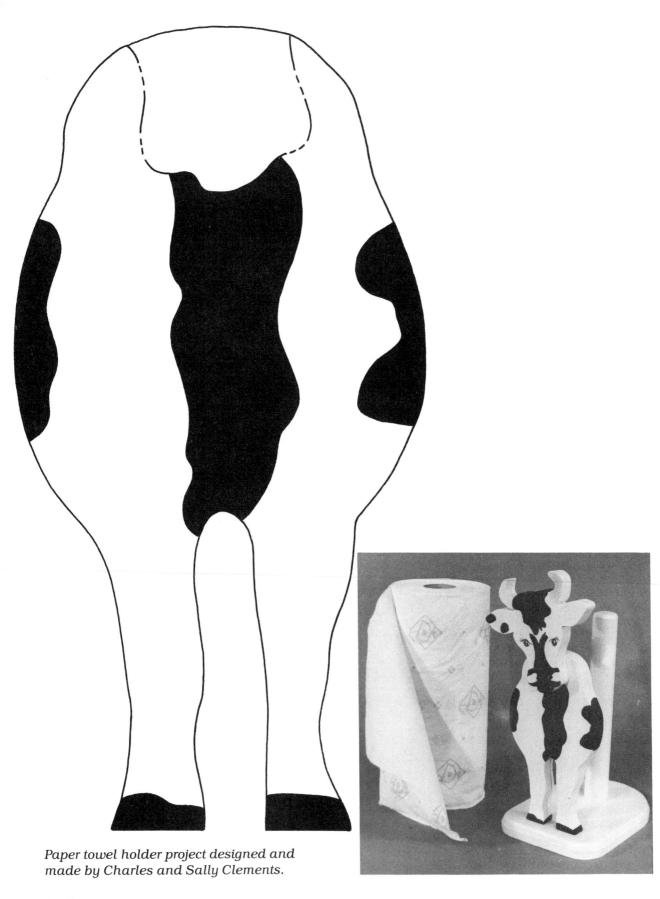

Paper towel holder project designed and made by Charles and Sally Clements.

Plaques and Silhouettes

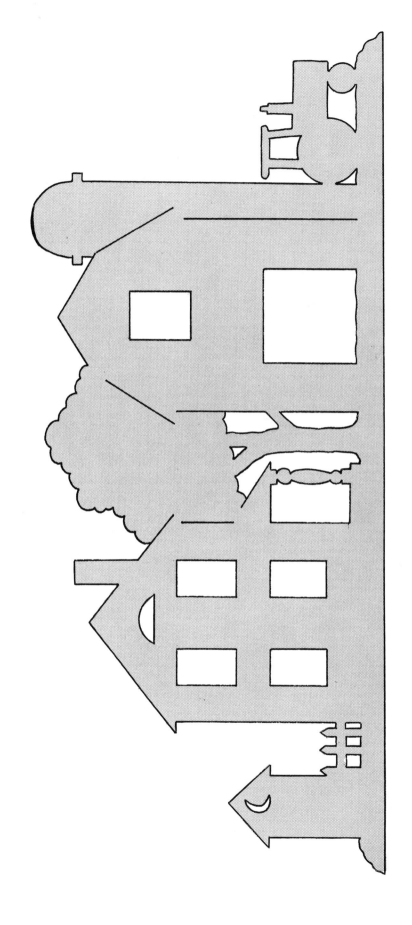

A

B

A

B

135

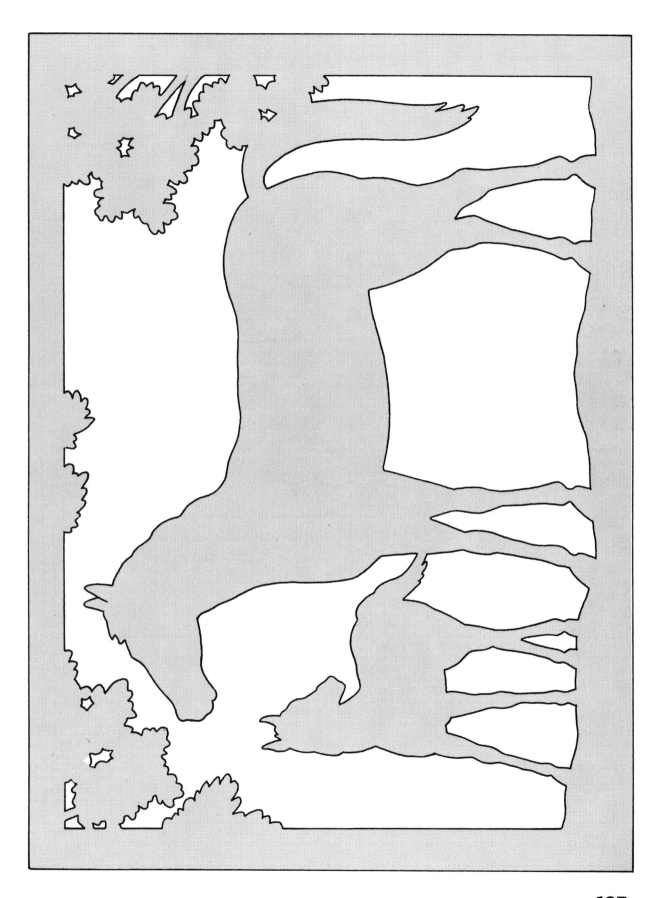

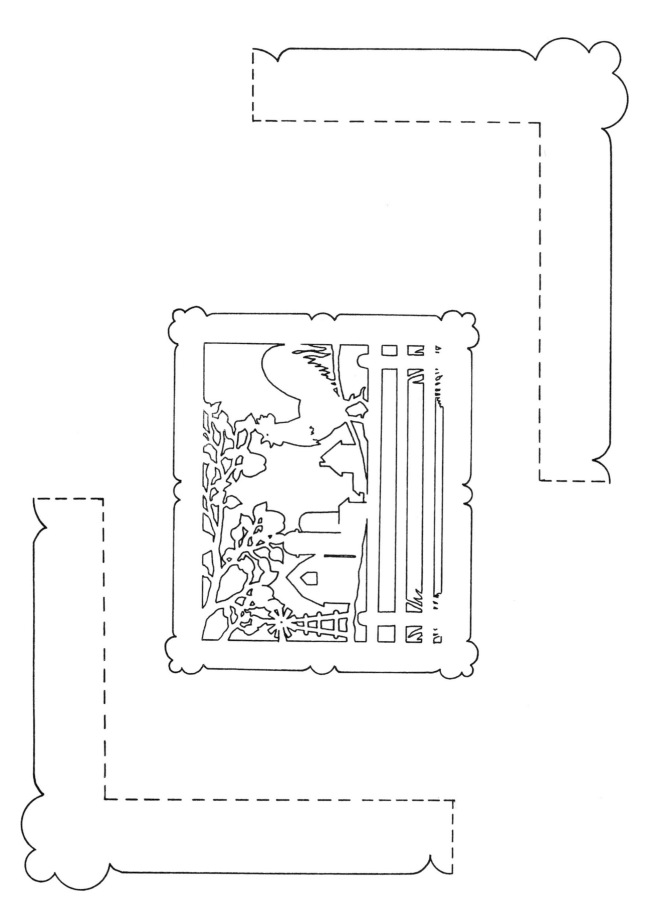

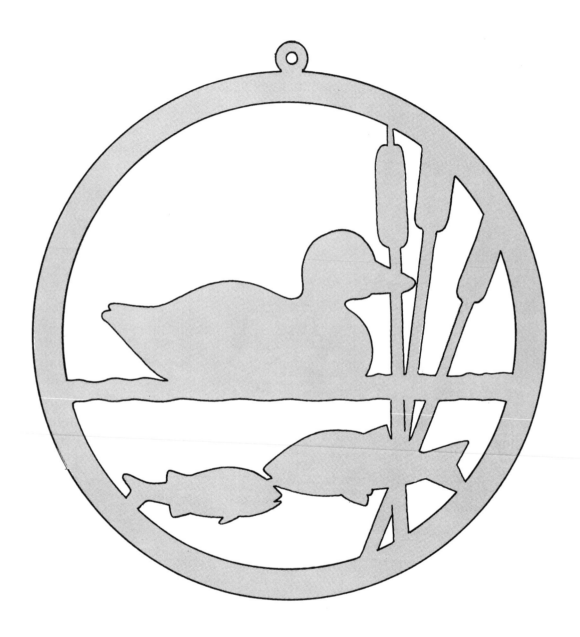

Letter Holder

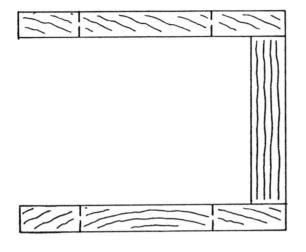

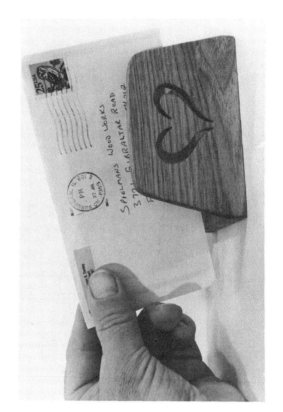

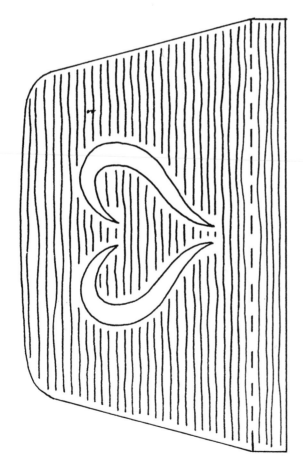

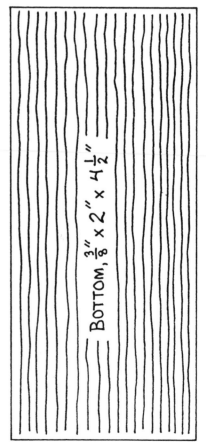

BOTTOM, $\frac{3}{8}$" x 2" x $4\frac{1}{2}$"

Letter and Key Holder

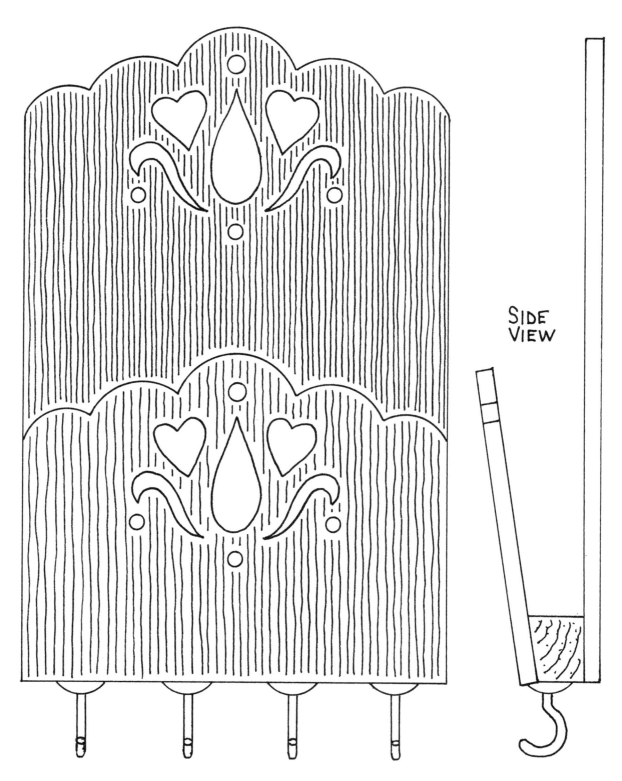

SIDE
VIEW

Kitchen Utensils

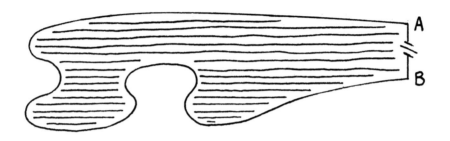

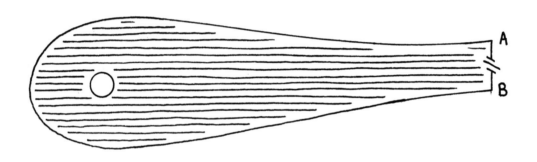

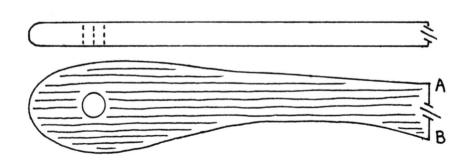

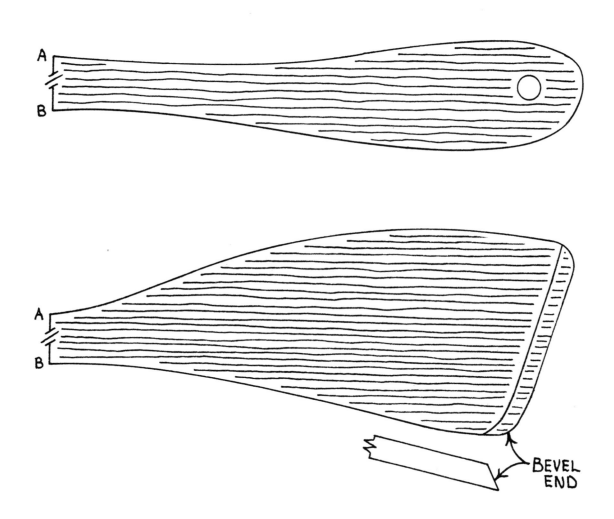

A

B

BEVEL
END

TAPER BLADE

A

B

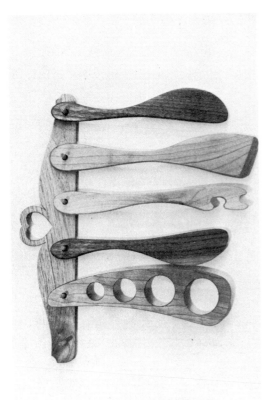

Wooden kitchen utensils and wall holder. From left: Pasta measurer, spreader, oven push-pull, and scraper.

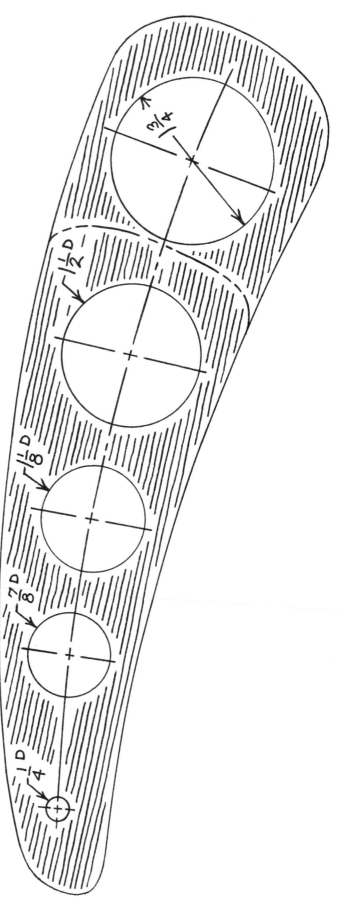

$\frac{3}{4}$

$\frac{1}{2}D$

$\frac{1}{8}D$

$\frac{7}{8}D$

$\frac{1}{4}D$

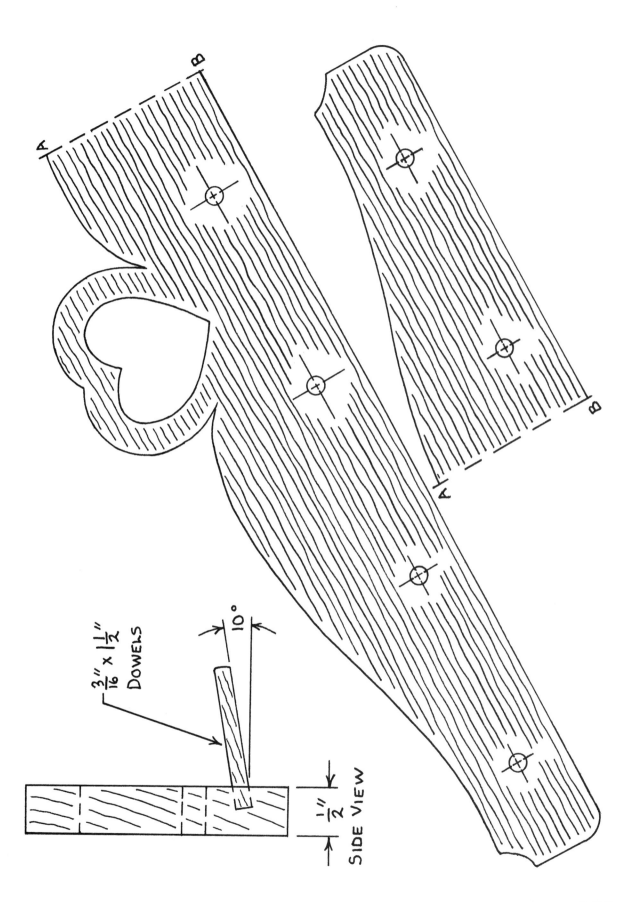

$\frac{3''}{16} \times 1\frac{1}{2}''$ Dowels

10°

$\frac{1''}{2}$

Side View

147

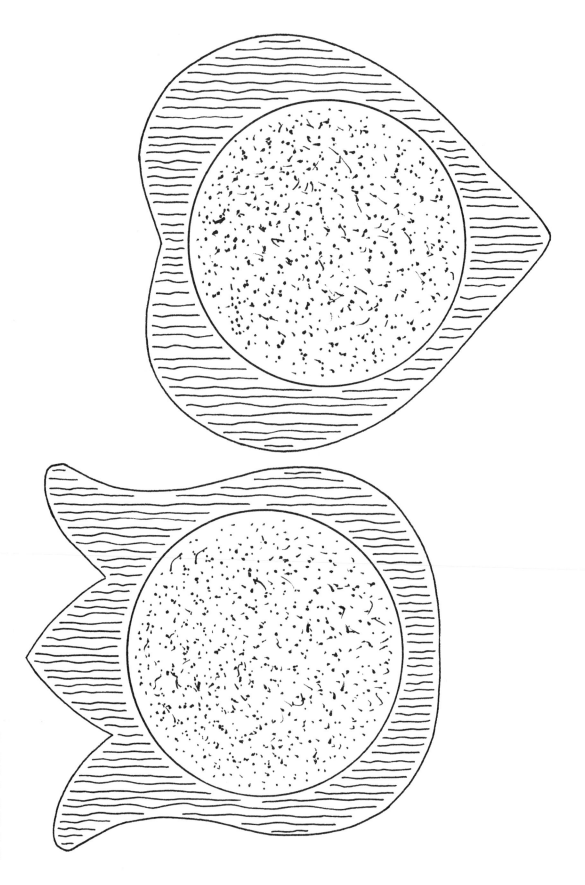

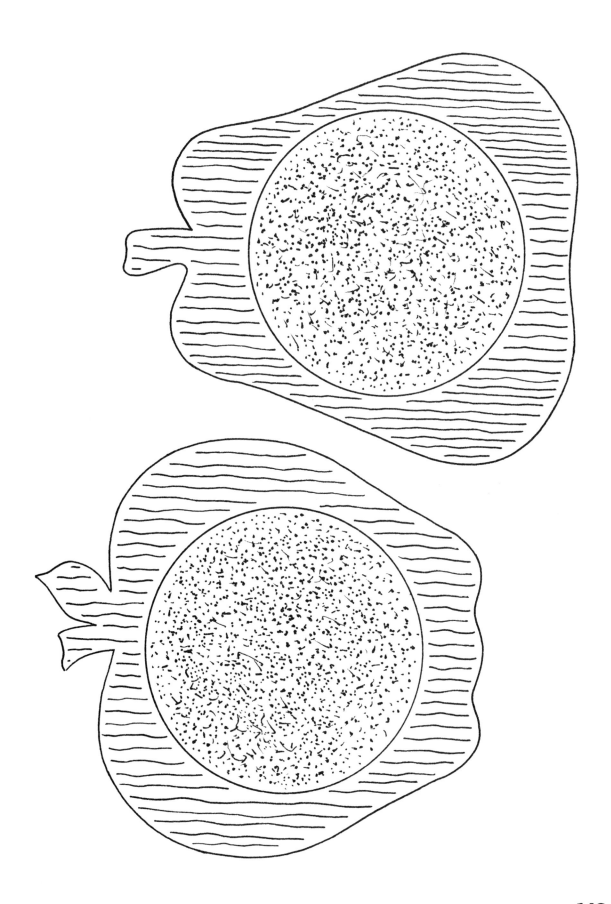

Country coasters have ⅛″ thick cork inserts.

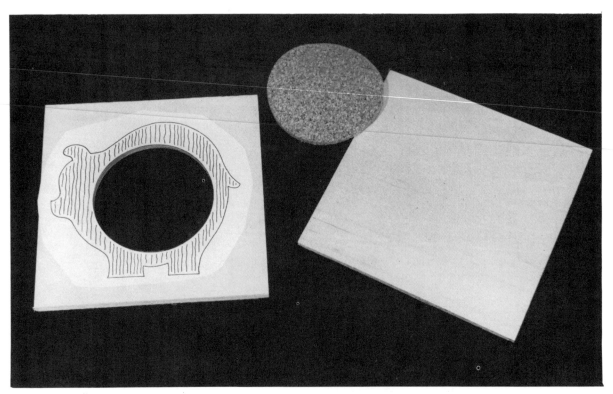

Coasters are made from two layers of ¼″ thick plywood. The opening in the piece on the left is cut out first, and then this piece glued to the back before cutting out the outline in both.

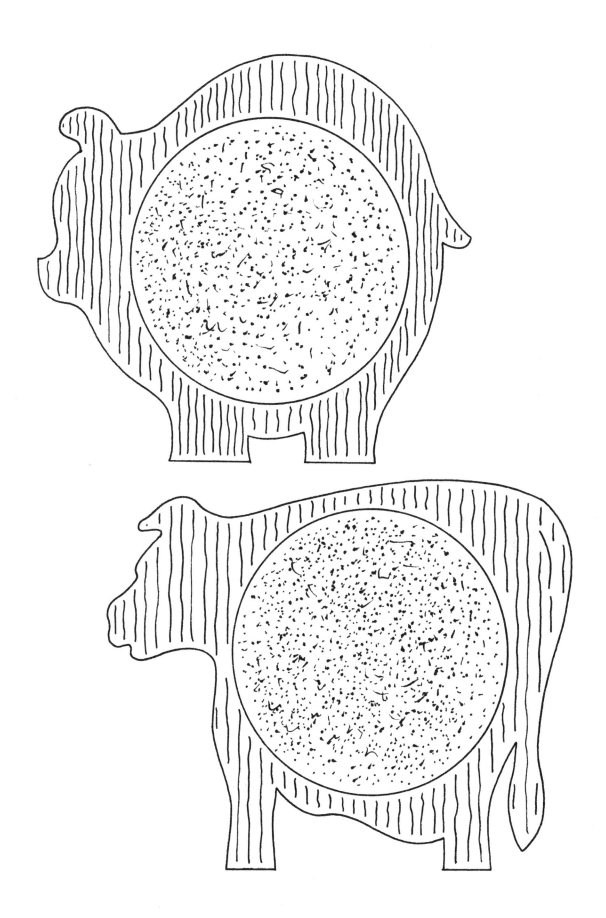

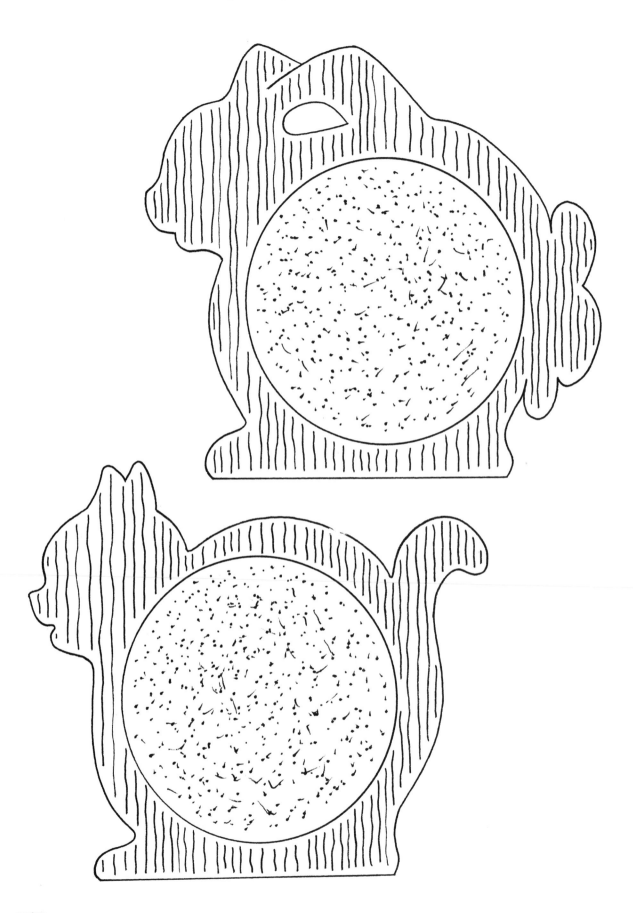

152

Switch Plates

The pierce-cut plate on the left is also stenciled. The other pieces have glued on overlays.

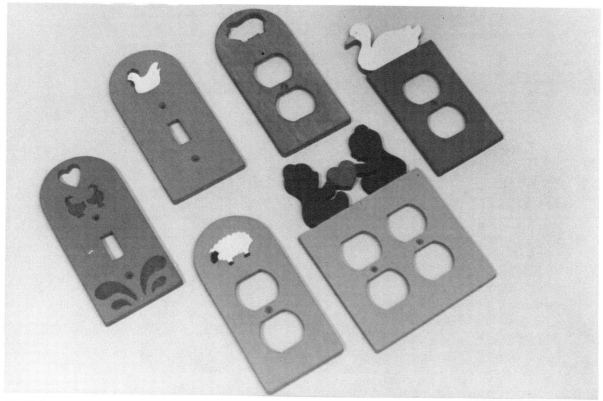

Switch and receptacle plates decorated with a variety of overlaid and pierce-cut designs.

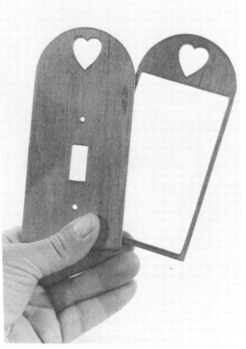

Rear view of a typical two-piece switch plate.

For best results switch plates should be made in two layers of thin plywood as shown. The rear frame makes for a tighter fit against the wall.

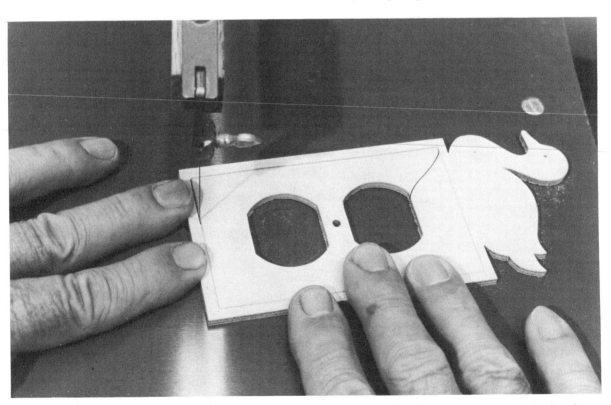

Cut both layers (stacked) at the same time, and then cut out the frame opening in the back piece separately.

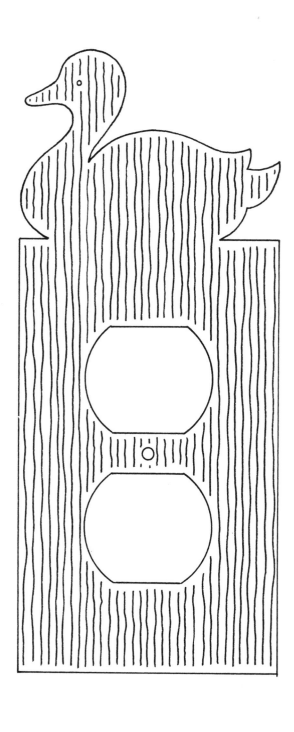
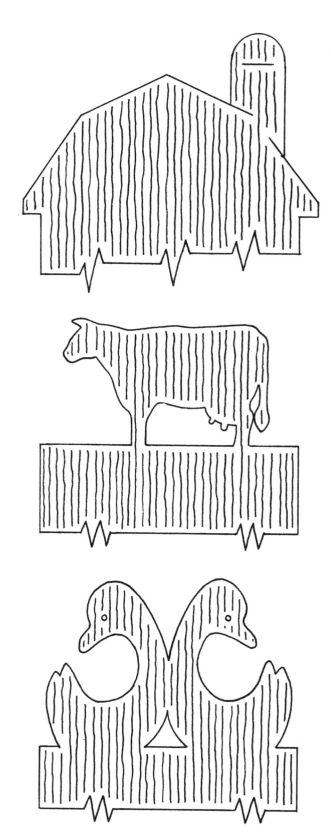

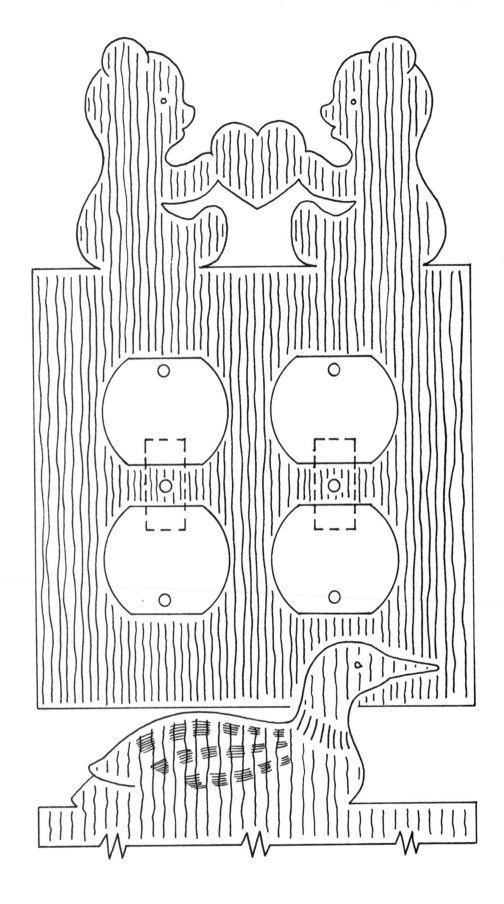

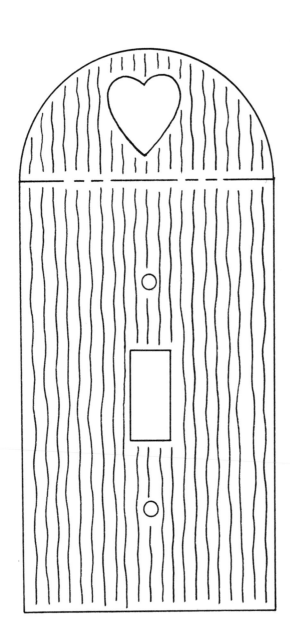

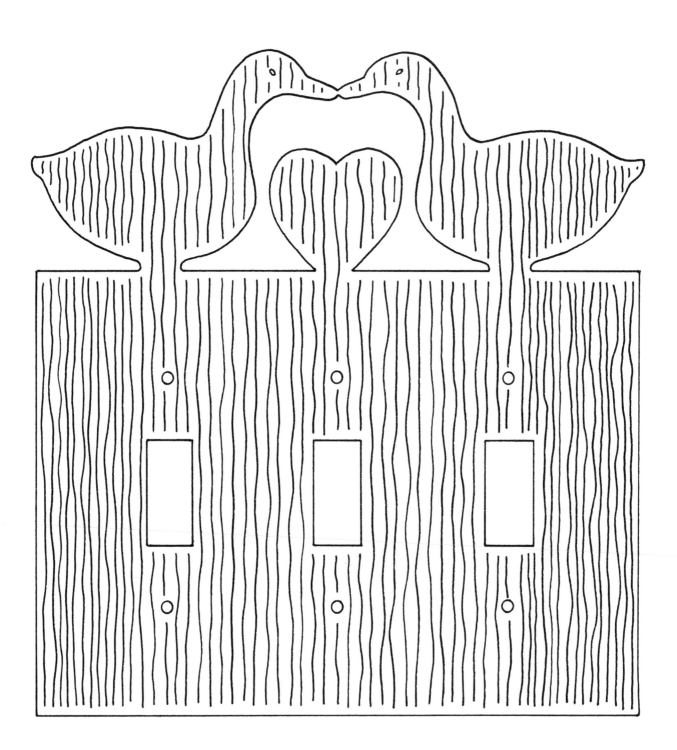

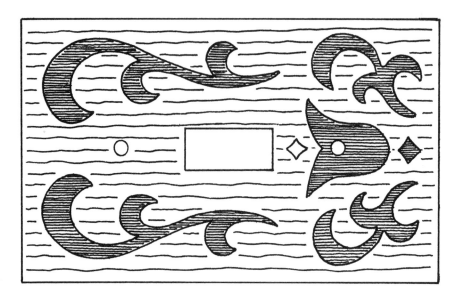

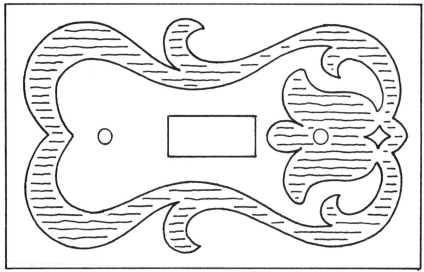

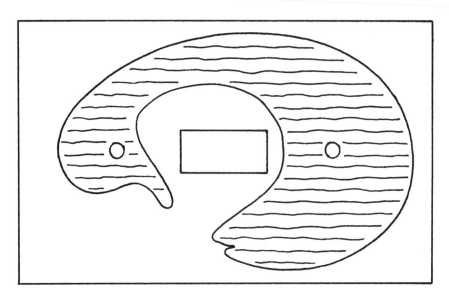

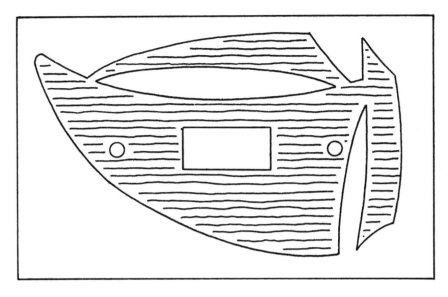

Boxes

Candle wall box.

Dry and silk flower box made from ¼" thick butternut.

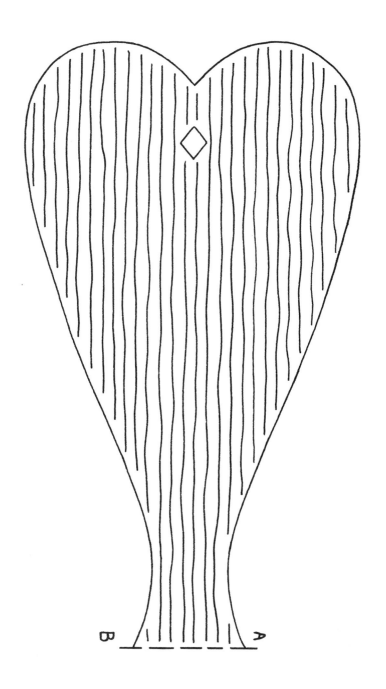

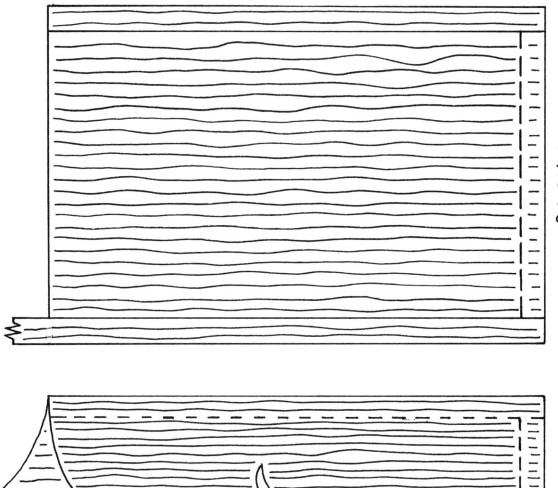

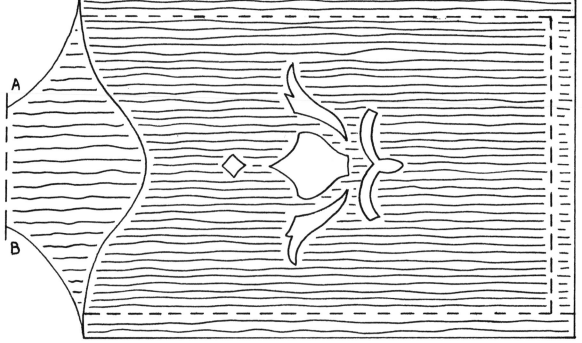

A

B

168

169

Match Boxes

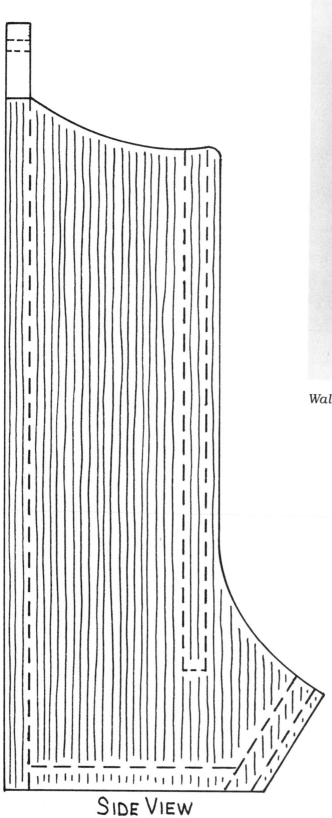

SIDE VIEW

Wall match box.

FRONT VIEW

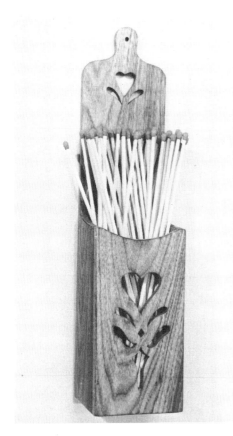

Wall box for long stick matches.

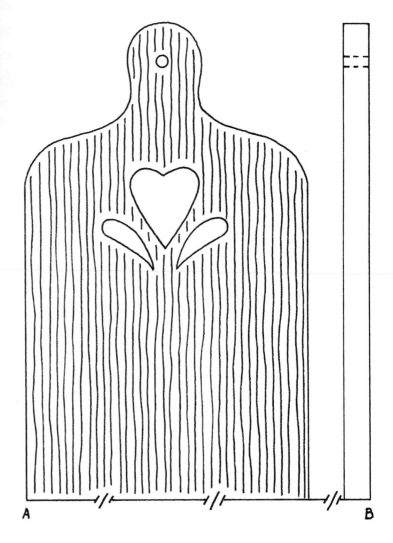

A

B

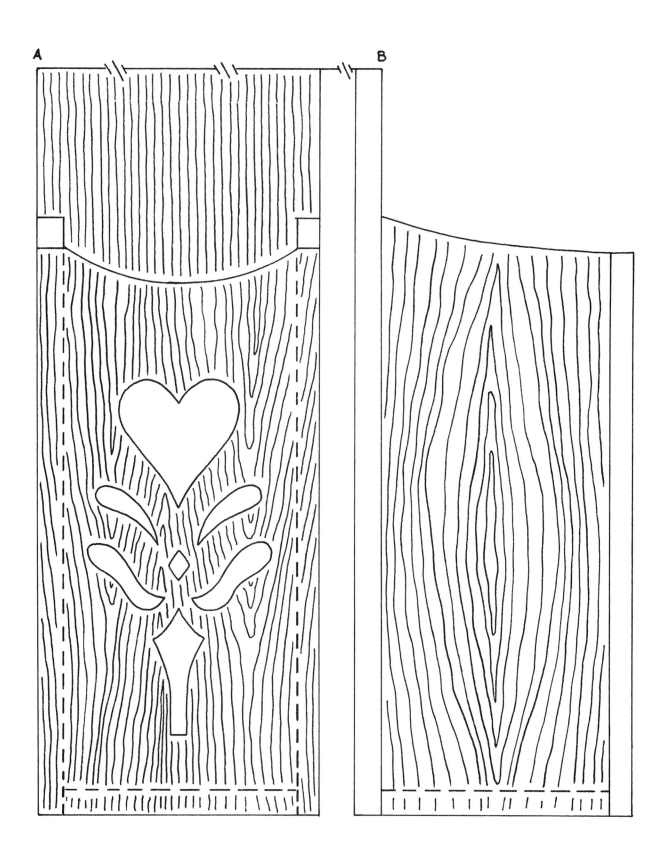

A

B

Shelves

A collector shelf made from ¼" thick wormy butternut.

Miniatures or collectibles shelf.

Wall shelf of ¼" thick butternut.

Wall shelf made of ¼" thick wormy butternut.

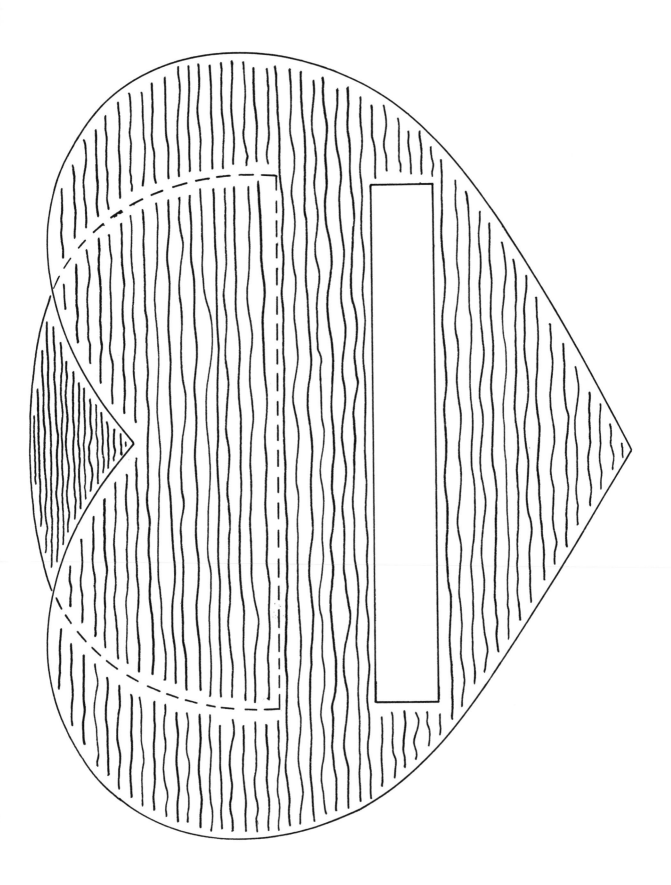

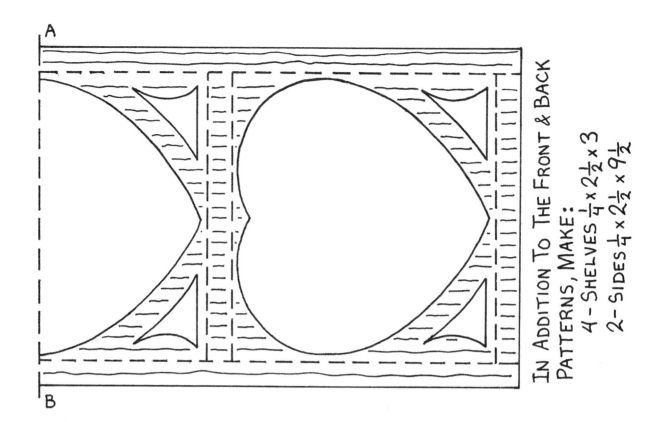

In Addition To The Front & Back Patterns, Make:

4 – Shelves $\frac{1}{4} \times 2\frac{1}{2} \times 3$

2 – Sides $\frac{1}{4} \times 2\frac{1}{2} \times 9\frac{1}{2}$

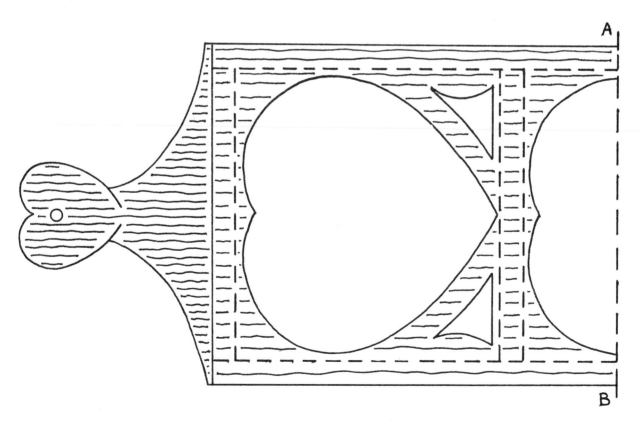

178

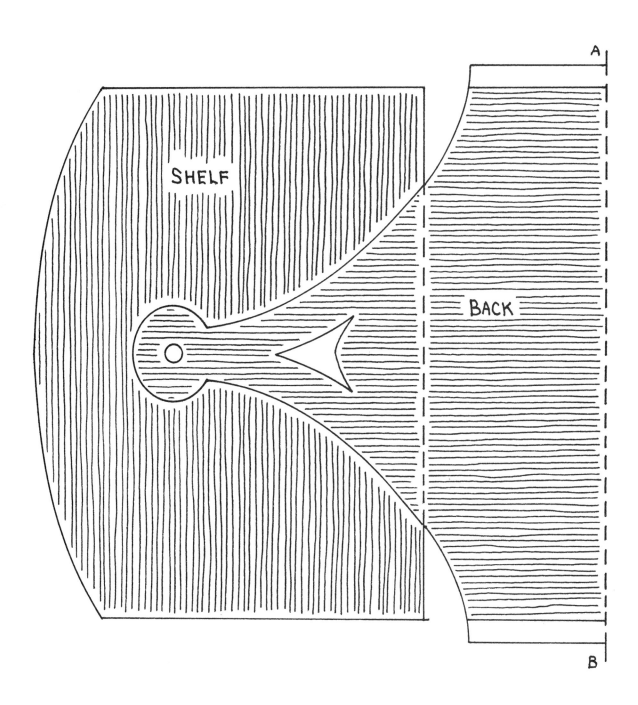

A

SHELF

BACK

B

179

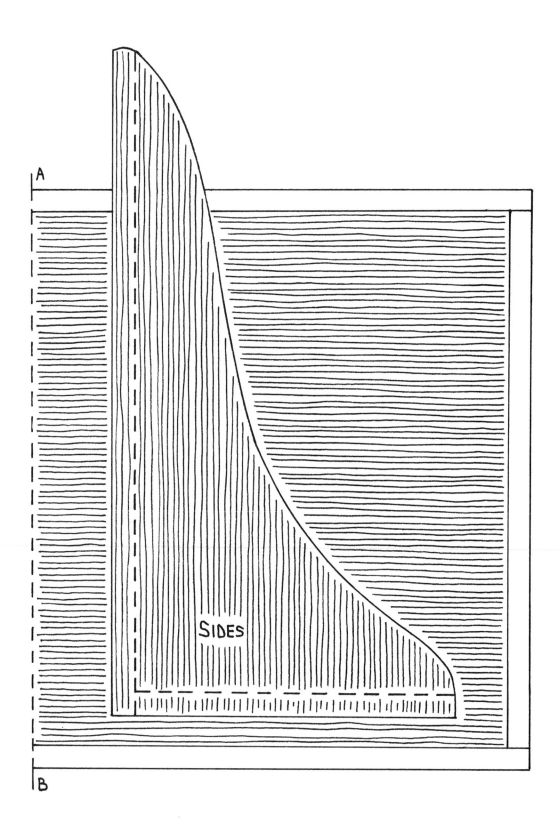

SIDES

A

B

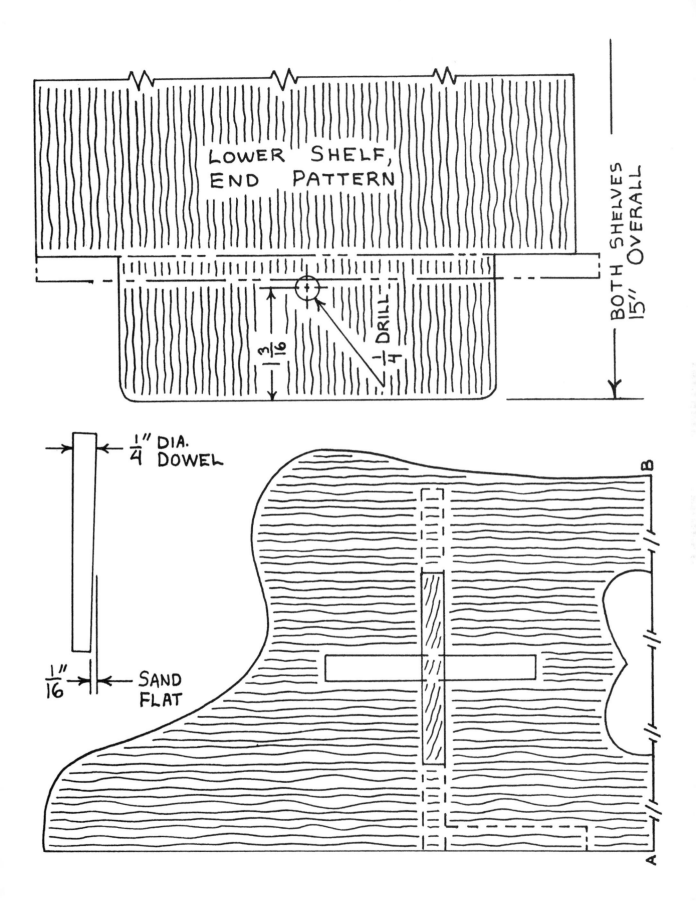

LOWER SHELF,
END PATTERN

BOTH SHELVES
15" OVERALL

$\frac{3}{16}$

$\frac{1}{4}$ DRILL

$\frac{1}{4}$" DIA.
DOWEL

$\frac{1}{16}$"

SAND
FLAT

B

A

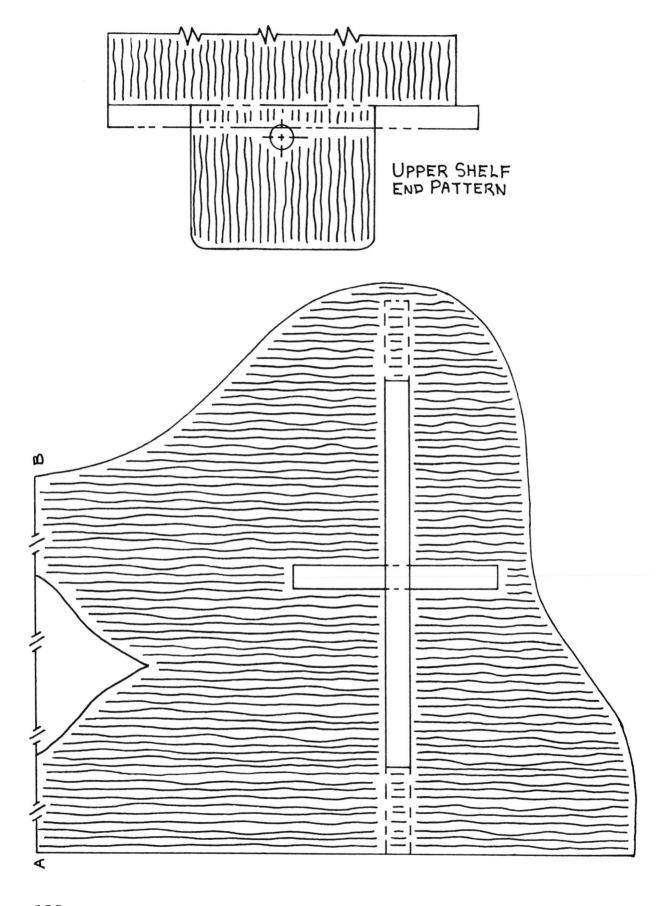

UPPER SHELF
END PATTERN

ABCDEF
GHIJKL
MNOPQ
RSTUV
WXYZ
1234567890

Alphabets

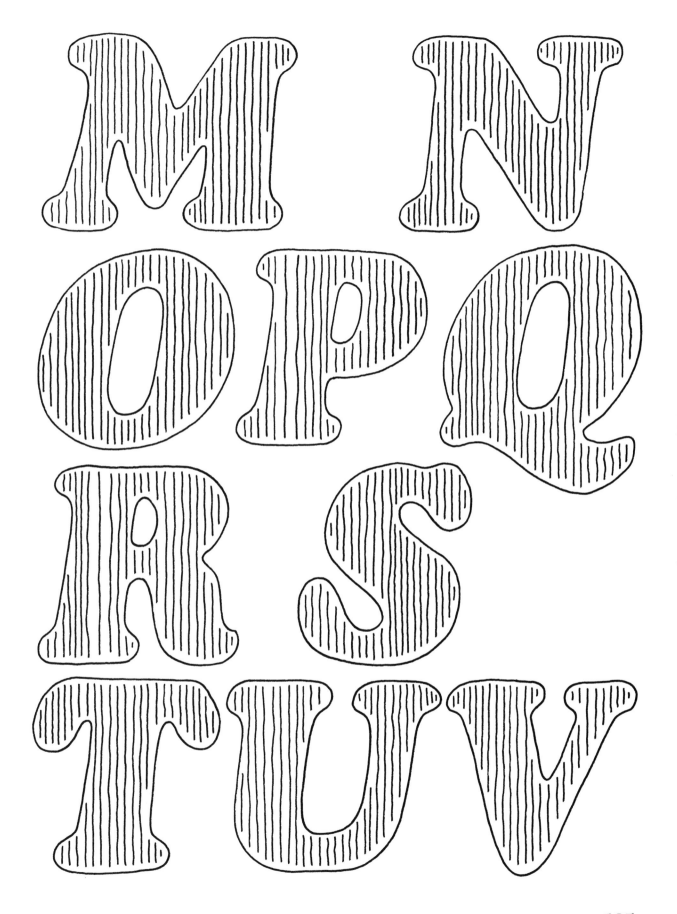

ABCDEF
GHIJKL
MNOPQR
STUVWX
YZ

1234567
890 &

About The Authors

Patrick Spielman's love of wood began when, as a child, he transformed fruit crates into toys. Now this prolific and innovative woodworker is respected worldwide as a teacher and author.

His most famous contribution to the woodworking field has been his perfection of a method to season green wood with polyethylene glycol 1000 (PEG). He went on to invent, manufacture, and distribute the PEG-Thermovat chemical seasoning system.

During his many years as a shop instructor in Wisconsin, Spielman published manuals, teaching guides, and more than 14 popular books, including *Modern Wood Technology*, a college text. He also wrote six educational series on wood technology, tool use, processing techniques, design, and wood-product planning.

Author of the best-selling *Router Handbook* (over 200,000 copies sold), Spielman has served as editorial consultant to a professional magazine, and his products, techniques, and many books have been featured in numerous periodicals.

This pioneer of new ideas and inventor of countless jigs, fixtures, and designs used throughout the world is a unique combination of expert woodworker and brilliant teacher—all of which endear him to his many readers and to his publisher.

At Spielmans Wood Works in the woods of northern Door County, Wisconsin, he and his family create and sell some of the most durable and popular furniture products and designs available.

Sherri Spielman Valitchka is the co-author, along with her father, Patrick, of *Alphabets and Designs for Wood Signs*. Sherri's interest in art, crafts and photography began when she was a child. She received professional training in graphic communications and now works as a graphic artist for an advertising agency in Milwaukee, Wisconsin.

Should you wish to write Pat or Sherri, please forward your letters to Sterling Publishing Company, Inc.

CHARLES NURNBERG
STERLING PUBLISHING COMPANY, INC.

Current Books by Patrick Spielman

Alphabets and Designs for Wood Signs. 50 alphabet patterns, plans for many decorative designs, the latest on hand carving, routing, cutouts, and sandblasting. Pricing data. Photo gallery (4 pages in color) of wood signs by professionals from across the U.S. Over 200 illustrations. 128 pages.

Carving Large Birds. Spielman and renowned woodcarver Bill Dehos show how to carve a fascinating array of large birds. All of the tools and basic techniques that are used are discussed in depth, and hundreds of photos, illustrations, and patterns are provided for carving graceful swans, majestic eagles, comical-looking penguins, a variety of owls, and scores of other birds. Oversized. 16 pages in full color. 192 pages.

Carving Wild Animals: Life-Size Wood Figures. Spielman and renowned woodcarver Bill Dehos show how to carve more than 20 magnificent creatures of the North American wild. A cougar, black bear, prairie dog, squirrel, raccoon, and fox are some of the life-size animals included. Step-by-step, photo-filled instructions and multiple-view patterns, plus tips on the use of tools, wood selection, finishing, and polishing help you bring each animal to life. Oversized. Over 300 photos; 16 pages in full color. 240 pages.

Gluing & Clamping. A thorough, up-to-date examination of one of the most critical steps in woodworking. Spielman explores the features of every type of glue—from traditional animal-hide glues to the newest epoxies—the clamps and tools needed, the bonding properties of different wood species, safety tips, and all techniques from edge-to-edge and end-to-end gluing to applying plastic laminates. Also included is a glossary of terms. Over 500 illlustrations. 256 pages.

Making Country-Rustic Wood Projects. Hundreds of photos, patterns, and detailed scaled drawings reveal construction methods, woodworking techniques, and Spielman's professional secrets for making indoor and outdoor furniture in the distinctly attractive Country-Rustic style. Covered are all aspects of furniture making from choosing the best wood for the job to texturing smooth boards. Among the dozens of projects are mailboxes, cabinets, shelves, coffee tables, weather vanes, doors, panelling, plant stands and many other durable and economical pieces. 400 illustrations. 4 pages in full color. 164 pages.

Making Wood Decoys. A clear step-by-step approach to the basics of decoy carving. This book is abundantly illustrated with closeup photos for designing, selecting, and obtaining woods; tools; feather detailing; painting; and finishing of decorative and working decoys. Six different professional decoy artists are featured. Photo gallery (4 pages in full color) along with numerous detailed plans for various popular decoys. 160 pages.

Making Wood Signs. Designing, selecting woods and tools, and every process through finishing are clearly covered. Hand-carved, power-carved, routed, and sandblasted processes in small to huge signs are presented. Foolproof guides for professional letters and ornaments. Hundreds of photos (4 pages in full color). Lists sources for supplies and special tooling. 144 pages.

Realistic Decoys. Spielman and master carver Keith Bridenhagen reveal their successful techniques for carving, feather-texturing, painting, and finishing wood decoys. Details that you can't find elsewhere—anatomy, attitudes, markings, and the easy step-by-step approach to perfect delicate procedures—make this book invaluable. Includes listings for contests, shows, and sources of tools and supplies. 274 closeup photos, 28 in color. 224 pages.

Router Handbook. With nearly 600 illustrations of every conceivable bit, attachment, jig, and fixture, plus every possible operation, this definitive guide has revolutionized router applications. It begins with safety and maintenance tips, then forges ahead into all aspects of dovetailing, free-handing, advanced duplication, and more. Details for over 50 projects are included. 224 pages.

Router Jigs & Techniques. A practical encyclopedia of information, covering the latest equipment to use with your router, it describes all the newest of commercial routing machines, along with jigs, bits, and other aids and devices. The book not only provides invaluable tips on how to determine the router and bits best suited to your needs, but tells you how to get the most out of your equipment once it is bought. Over 800 photos and illustrations. 384 pages.

Scroll Saw Handbook. This companion volume to *Scroll Saw Pattern Book* covers the essentials of this versatile tool, including the basics (how scroll saws work, blades to use, etc.) and the advantages and disadvantages of the general types and specific brand-name models available on the market. All cutting techniques are detailed, including compound and bevel sawing, making inlays, reliefs, and recesses, cutting metals and other non-woods, and marquetry. There's even a section on transferring patterns to wood! Over 500 illustrations. 256 pages.

Scroll Saw Fretwork Patterns. This companion book to *Scroll Saw Fretwork Techniques and Projects* features over 200 fabulous full-size fretwork patterns. These patterns include the most popular classic designs of the past, plus an array of imaginative contemporary ones. Choose from a variety of numbers, signs, brackets, animals, miniatures, and silhouettes, and many more. 256 pages.

Scroll Saw Fretwork Techniques and Projects. Spielman and master woodworker Reidle team up to make fretwork a quick and easy skill for anyone with access to a scroll saw, explaining every intricate detail in easy-to-follow instructions, photos, and drawings. Patterns for dozens of projects make it easy for any scroll saw user to master these designs. 232 pages (8 in color).

Scroll Saw Pattern Book. This companion book to *Scroll Saw Handbook* contains over 450 workable patterns for making wall plaques, refrigerator magnets, candle holders, pegboards, jewelry, ornaments, shelves, brackets, picture frames, signboards, and many more projects. Beginners and experienced scroll sawyers alike will be challenged. 256 pages.

Scroll Saw Puzzle Patterns. 80 full-size patterns for jigsaw puzzles, standup puzzles and inlay puzzles. With meticulous attention to detail, Patrick and Patricia Spielman provide instruction and step-by-step photos, along with tips on tools and wood selections, for making standup puzzles in the shape of dinosaurs, camels, hippopotamuses, alligators—even a family of elephants! Inlay puzzle patterns include basic shapes, numbers, an accurate piece-together map of the United States and a host of other colorful, educational and enjoyable games for children. 8 pages of color. 256 pages.

Spielman's Original Scroll Saw Patterns. Patrick Spielman has teamed up with his wife, Patricia, on this all-new book of scroll saw patterns, with projects covering over 30 different categories, including teddy bears, dinosaurs, musical cutouts, sports figures, dancers, and a variety of mobiles. Each step is clearly spelled out, with hundreds of photos and drawings that show you how to flop, repeat, and crop each design for thousands of variations. 224 pages.

Working Green Wood with PEG. Covers every process for making beautiful, inexpensive projects from green wood without cracking, splitting, or warping. Hundreds of clear photos and drawings show every step from obtaining the raw wood through shaping, treating, and finishing your PEG-treated projects. 175 unusual project ideas. Lists supply sources. 160 pages.

INDEX

For information on how you can have *Better Homes & Gardens*
magazine delivered to your door, write to:
Robert Austin, P.O. Box 4536, Des Moines, IA 50336.